Stand Up for the Gospel is a clari

manipulation through false teachings about the Kingdom of God and to focus on the good news of our Lord Jesus Christ that transforms unto eternal life. I recommend this book to fellow church leaders, pastors, lay leaders, seminary students, and Sunday school teachers, as well as those who seek encouragement to continue on the path of truth – not only in Africa but all over the world.

—Most Rev Daniel Okoh, General Superintendent of Christ Holy Church International and International Chairman of Organization of African Instituted Churches

The call of Jude to "contend for the faith" is as legitimate for us today as it was back then; it cannot be ignored. The growth and expansion of the church in Africa today speaks to a biblical truth in which the God of all grace chooses that which is foolish, weak, low, and despised in the world, to shame the wise, strong, and high. Amoafo delivers a bold call for consistent expression of faith that bridges the gap between growth and impact. This is a timely work of great relevance, and we must be grateful for this prophetic study.

—Rev Prof J. Kwabena Asamoah-Gyadu, Baeta-Grau Professor of African Christianity and Pentecostal Theology, President of Trinity Theological Seminary, Ghana

Amoafo succinctly exposits the letter of Jude to expose the false "men of God" in present-day Africa who preach a false gospel and practise similar ungodliness and immorality. True to Scripture and unflinchingly practical, Amoafo is not ashamed to allow the message of Jude to wear African clothes and African shoes. Amoafo vividly shows how Jude lays out a battle plan for fighting such false teachings which centres on the unmerited grace of God found in Jesus Christ. Byang Kato, to whom the book is dedicated, would be most proud of his spiritual son in the Lord! Every African Christian and pastor ought to read this book and find true freedom in Christ.

—**Bishop Martin Morrison, Chairman of**
The Gospel Coalition Africa, Bishop of REACH SA

An imaginative, stimulating, and profound exposition of the New Testament letter of Jude. Amoafo weaves examples from world history, illustrations from various African countries, and above all copious biblical passages and personal experiences to present authentic Christianity, along with a robust critique of various contemporary distortions, notably the prosperity gospel. Highly recommended for leaders and lay of all denominations.

—**Prof Paul Gifford, Emeritus Professor of Religion,**
SOAS, University of London, and author of
Christianity, Development and Modernity in Africa

The Lord graciously raises up a prophet for the church in each season. Amoafo's convicting message is one such prophecy. Amoafo could very well be helming a movement that returns the fastest growing branches of Christianity to their rightful biblical roots.

Stand Up for the Gospel deserves wide readership *and action*. We ignore this message to our peril, and especially to the future of Christianity in Africa. *Stand Up for the Gospel* compels a re-orientation in our discipleship.

—**Rev Dr Casely Baiden Essamuah,**
Secretary of the Global Christian Forum

Amoafo's book has come at a critical time when "godless men" propagate many false doctrines, distorting the truth of the gospel of Jesus Christ for their selfish gain. Intrigued by how Jude responded to false teachings, Amoafo addresses the distortions and the negation of the gospel in the church in Africa. I strongly recommend this book to leaders, ministers of the gospel, lecturers, theological students, and Christians, who love the church and are enthusiastic to guard the truth of the gospel of Jesus Christ, who want to see the church reflect God's Kingdom on earth.

—**Prof James Nkansah-Obrempong, Professor of Systematic Theology and Ethics and Dean, Nairobi Evangelical Graduate School of Theology (AIU), Kenya**

Amoafo's experiences both in Ghana and Kenya give him great perspective on some of the distorted teachings across the continent. While the innovation of African Independent Churches addressed the African worldview of the supernatural, it created room for specially anointed teachers and their doctrines to be accepted uncritically. In desperate hope for better economic prospects, many people become open to manipulation through the teachings of the prosperity gospel. Ironically, leaders become wealthy while their members remain poor. In this book, Amoafo calls for a return to biblical teaching and preaching. I highly commend this book.

—**Rev Dr Linda Ochola-Adolwa, Church Partnerships Coordinator for International Justice Mission, Kenya**

Amoafo issues a valuable, timely warning about the prosperity gospel. He lets the biblical text speak powerfully, illustrated again and again by real-life examples he encountered during his doctoral research for this book. He also provides fruitful positive stories of believers in Africa who have pursued the truth of the gospel, as urged by Jude. The tone is balanced and measured, as the author lets Jude point to better paths for biblical faithfulness. Readers will find the study questions that accompany each chapter especially helpful for sensitive reflection.

—Dr Paul Bowers, editor, *Christian Reflection
in Africa: Review and Engagement*

Amoafo puts forward precious nuggets gleaned from the book of Jude that can help the church in Africa to move from its serious theological flaws to a place of hope, truth, and power.

The book offers rich content on how to contend for the faith and helpful guidelines for anyone who has strayed to return to the gospel truth. It comes in handy as a valuable resource to help the church in Africa, currently growing numerically, to grow spiritually too. I strongly endorse and recommend it to all Christians, pastors, and Bible school teachers in Africa and beyond.

—Rev Dr Abraham Obeng-Amoako, Pastor and
Former Head of Operations, Assemblies of God, Ghana

Standing up for the gospel is synonymous with standing up for Christ since Christ is essentially the gospel. The author has provided the general readership, especially Bible students, the local church pastor and academic faculty with an easy-to-read theological book for the church in Africa. The discussion questions amply position the book for good theological reflections.

—Rev Prof Lt Col Vincent Setsoafia, Senior Pastor of House of
Integrity, Adjunct faculty of Assemblies of God Theological
Seminary and West Africa Advanced School of Theology

While providing an insightful expository study of the book of Jude grounded in its historical context and presented in a winsome and relevant manner for the church today, Amoafo offers many illustrations from and insights into the contemporary church of Africa. He calls the church in Africa and globally to proclaim uncompromisingly and to live unswervingly the authentic gospel, centred on the life, death, resurrection, and return of the Lord Jesus Christ.

—**Dr Douglas P. Lowenberg, Chair of the Bible/Theology Department, Pan-Africa Theological Seminary**

After the manner of Byang Kato, a widely acclaimed advocate of doctrinal purity and orthodoxy in Africa, Amoafo takes on all manner of false teachings and calls Africa to return to the purity of the faith and doctrine. Spirited, well-written, and based on Amoafo's doctoral research, this study will be widely read and talked about throughout Africa and will certainly have an impact.

—**Prof Canon Aloo Osotsi Mojola, St Paul's University, Limuru, Kenya, former Africa Translation Coordinator for United Bible Societies**

Amoafo takes the threat of the so-called prosperity gospel head-on, proving from Scripture that this is no gospel at all but rather a dangerous counterfeit that deprives people of the blessing of the true gospel. *Stand Up for the Gospel* is expertly written, masterfully weaving sound biblical teaching with heart-warming stories of real people affected by the prosperity doctrine and those battling it. While it raises the alarm, it also chronicles battles won. It is ultimately a book about hope, full of wisdom and practical advice. This book is a must-read for every Christian.

—**Dr Audrey Julia Walegwa Mbogho, Associate Professor of Computer Science, United States International University – Africa**

Following my 12 years of mission and 14 years of related ministry and work in Africa, this book was close to my heart. The book's insights and examples will really resonate with the reader. The prosperity doctrine is exploiting the poor and vulnerable, which is why I warmly recommend this book to anyone. It is refreshing to have this clear, logical, biblical explanation.

I pray this book will reach missionaries, Bible colleges, theological institutions, and anyone attracted or confused by the prosperity doctrine. I hope that, by reading this book, all pastors will reawaken to their responsibility to teach their flock what the Word says. Jude and this book conclude with practical applications on how to protect ourselves and the church from destructive false doctrines. If we stand up for the gospel, God will keep us eternally safe from falling, and we will never stop praising him.

—**Ms Seintje Veldhuis, Leadership Coach,**
Former Africa Regional Director of Feed the Children

STAND UP
FOR THE
GOSPEL

Getting the Church
Back on Track

EMMANUEL KWASI AMOAFO

This book is dedicated to the memory of
Dr Byang Kato, the outstanding and inspiring
African Christian leader of an earlier generation,
who blazed the trail of contending in Africa for
the faith once for all delivered to the saints. In his
brief years in this world, Dr Byang Kato fought
tirelessly and bravely for the cause of the gospel
of Jesus Christ to ensure that African Christians
become, first and foremost, Christian Africans.
May the Lord continue to use Dr Kato's work to
restore to today's church in Africa the apostolic
faith of the early New Testament church that
turned its world upside down (Acts 17:6).

Kente cloth is featured on the book's back cover.
Weaving the colorful silk *kente* cloth is an ancient
tradition of the Ashanti people of Ghana.
The richly woven silk *kente* fabric was originally
used exclusively to dress kings and their royal courts.
Each block, pattern, and colour in the *kente* fabric
has a distinct name and meaning, and the
cloth often includes *adinkra* symbols.

Adinkra is an ancient set of traditional symbols
designed and used by the Akan people of Ghana.
The symbols represent concepts about their
understanding of God's power and presence,
popular proverbs and maxims, and they also record
historical events. Each chapter in this book begins
with a symbol and its meaning, corresponding
to the biblical theme of the chapter.

Aligning our cultures with the Bible
reminds us of Byang Kato's words,
"Let African Christians be Christian Africans."

CONTENTS

ACKNOWLEDGEMENTS

This book must have first been conceived in the heart of God and implanted in my mind and heart by his Holy Spirit because of the palpable sense of his continuous grace and mercy that have guided every step of writing the book. It is the almighty God, therefore, who must first be acknowledged and given overall credit for this book.

Without the blessing, love, support, and encouragement of my dear wife Esther, and my children, Kwame Anthony, Kwame Nkrumah, Yaa Henrika, Abena Mkawasi, and Kofi Emmanuel, completing this book would have probably taken a lot longer. I thank the Lord for their prayers, love, and continuing supportive and enduring encouragement.

Every book can only be successfully completed through the efforts of many people besides the author, and this book is no exception. I cannot thank enough, Hannah Rasmussen, my editor, for her brilliant, patient, and inspired work of suggesting changes, additions and subtractions to my original unwieldy and scholarly manuscript. Without her untiring, committed, and dedicated support and talented editorial work, this book would probably still be sitting in my library in its original form. The Lord enabled Hannah to catch the vision he had given me for the book, and together, the Holy Spirit guided us to bring the book to this final completed form.

This book is an adaptation of my PhD dissertation. Therefore, I once again acknowledge with much gratitude all the help I received from my local church community, my family in Ghana, the leaders of the churches in Ghana that I researched for the dissertation, the scholars and church leaders who have mentored and inspired me, my fellow students in my PhD cohort class, and above all, the wonderful, dedicated, and inspiring administrative and teaching team at Pan Africa Theological Seminary.

The whole village raises the African child, an old saying declares. Everyone mentioned above, and many others not mentioned, have all been part of the village that has nurtured, raised, and supported this book to bring it to its current completed form.

May the Lord richly bless you all, and may he use this book to accomplish his redemptive and transformative work in the lives of his people in Africa and beyond.

Learn from the Past

INTRODUCTION
TWO STORIES

This book is about two stories: the story of the church that Jude wrote to in the first century, and the story of our churches in Africa today. For several years I studied the history, the background, and the message of Jude for my doctorate. As I did so I came to realize that Jude held the key to solving the serious problem of departures from the gospel that we find in the church in Africa today.

I invite you to listen in on these two stories.

Story No. 1

A group of believers gathered in the atrium courtyard of a wealthy Christian's home one early Sunday evening. They had just finished singing and praying. A tall and handsome suntanned visitor rose to address this home church. The man's curly hair was greying at the temples, and he was dressed impeccably in the attire of his day.[1]

"As followers of Jesus Christ, we judge our own actions. No one can accuse us of sin by the standards of the Law of Moses or the moral order of creation. The so-called angels who gave the Law are against human beings. We reject their authority. The grace of God in Christ Jesus has set us free from being judged by those human moral codes. We are people who possess the Spirit. The Spirit gives us knowledge beyond ordinary human knowledge through dreams. What other authority do we need?"

Many of the listeners sat still, their full attention captured by the words of the speaker.

"Many churches in which we have taught are now living the free life. You can do the same. We thank you for receiving us to share in your fellowship meals. We are grateful for your great Christian hospitality and financial support. God will richly bless you all for this. We will continue to share our teachings and our visions with you to set you free completely in Christ."

As he finished, the man called his travelling ministry companion, who was seated in the front row, to address the gathering. This second man was younger, shorter, and more athletic-looking than the first man. With his more working-class appearance, many in the assembly identified with the second speaker. "Remember, we are people of the Spirit. As people of the Spirit, we have already been judged in Christ, so we face no future judgement from God."

Several listeners yelled, "Amen!"

"Because Jesus Christ has set us free from the Law of Moses all things are now permitted to us. Don't forget that food, alcohol, music, sex, and all other material things will pass away. What does God care about our diet or menu? What does he care about our sex lives? Don't you think he is concerned with important eternal spiritual matters, like our souls? We can enjoy life today because God has given us all things. We can have a life that is heaven on earth. We can have God's blessings *and* all the pleasures and freedom that this world has to offer. Praise the Lord!"

He closed his eyes and prayed in tongues, with his arms raised high. He ended his speech by saying, "The will of God is whatever the Spirit in you directs you to think, say, and do. We need to be free to enjoy life. I can tell you that I am inspired by the Spirit through my visions and dreams to live the free life. Our ecstatic experiences of the Spirit show us that we are free indeed."

As had happened over the past two weeks, the preaching by the two men produced a mixed response from the congregation. Some smiled and clapped their approval. One older lady, seated near the rear, whispered to the younger woman sitting next to her, "This sounds very different from what the apostles taught us."

The patron of the home offered a prayer to bless the communal meal that followed the service. He then invited the two preachers and five other elegantly dressed members of the assembly to join him in the smaller dining room adjoining the large living room for an elaborate feast. "God will surely bless you for your hospitality, brother," said the first preacher, smiling broadly. The less affluent members of the congregation were left behind in the atrium to provide for themselves as best they could.

After a while, the congregation heard loud drunken laughter from the smaller dining room and the voices of the beautiful mistresses who accompanied the men on their itinerant ministries.[2] Clearly, the two preachers practised what they preached.

Story No. 2

"Your victory as a Christian means that you need to reject all negative realities. Reject them. Refuse to speak about them. What you say is what you get. So do not pray about problems. You will only increase them by doing so because you are agreeing with Satan. God only wants good things for you. Have a positive confession. Pray what you desire. In my church back home, we never use the words 'for better, for worse' in any wedding ceremony. When you say 'for worse' you only give room for Satan to attack your marriage. I refused to sign the will my lawyer drew up because it read, 'after my death'. How can I call my death like that? We cannot die before our God-given 70 years or more. If you sow the right seeds, many of you will live to be 100 or more!"

On a Friday evening, the well-known visitor preached to a packed church auditorium in which air conditioning ensured everyone was comfortable. Thousands of people had seen the billboards across the African city advertising this *Heaven on Earth* conference. The speakers who smiled from the posters now sat on the stage, all attired in expensive designer clothing. One was the founder and senior pastor of the church. The other three men were itinerant preachers who had flown in from two African cities and one American city.

The speaker continued, "Listen, my dear brothers and sisters. Colonialism is long past, with the poverty it brought. We are no longer victims. God is our Father. He is very rich, and he wants his children to be rich in this life. Look at me. I live in a house worth hundreds of thousands of dollars. I own several cars of the latest model. I am successful. I am rich. I broke the forces of darkness over my life. I was born poor, yes, but today I am rich. You can be the same. Look at me. I am building a shopping mall and a 5-star hotel. I follow God's principles in the Bible. I sow and I reap. You can do the same. You can be a winner today."

The crowd cheered and clapped. "Amen! Hallelujah!"

"Jesus was born poor, but he became a winner. Look, the Bible tells us that they fought over his designer clothes as he hung on the cross. Tell your neighbour next to you, 'One day they will fight over my designer clothes!' None of you were born lower than Jesus. Look at where he is today – he is on the throne. Do you want to get on the throne God has created for you? Then you need to pay the same price Jesus paid. You must sacrifice. You must sow real seeds into real ministries of great men of God. No cheap stuff! Cheap stuff results in cheap results! Jesus became poor so that we might become rich. We are

> Jude's brief epistle is the strongest and most direct NT rejection of false teaching.

not meant to suffer. God has not destined us for anything but riches and perfect health. Suffering, pain, and poverty are not the portion of a true believer because Jesus died to purchase those things for us."

The rest of the speakers emphasized that God is able and willing to open the heavens to pour out his blessings of material wealth, health, and deliverance from witchcraft for Africans today. The praise team led lively singing as the conference attendants danced several times to an offering box in the front of the church to "sow their seeds."

One Story

These two stories above present scenes that are familiar in many of our churches across Africa today. You may need to read closely to see which story is from the church of the first-century world of Jude (the first story) and which one is from the 21st-century world of the African church today (the second story).

That is because these two stories are really a single story of teaching that has veered off from the gospel of Jesus Christ. Both scenarios demonstrate serious distortions, negations, and departures from the gospel of Jesus Christ. I am familiar with the first-century church world of Jude through my theological studies, and I am familiar with the 21st-century world of the African church through my teaching and preaching ministry.

Throughout the centuries, the church has almost always been troubled by teaching that negates, distorts, or departs from the gospel of Jesus Christ. Christ himself warned his followers to beware of false prophets and false messiahs (Matthew 7:15-23; 24:4, 23-26). This is also the reason why in their epistles Paul and the apostles took up such considerable space to warn the early church about false teachings (2 Corinthians 11–12; Galatians; Colossians; 1 Timothy; 2 Timothy; 2 John; 2 Peter). Even in the days of the Old Testament (OT), God's people had to contend with individuals and groups, some even from among their own ranks, who wanted to turn them away from following God.

Jude refers to them as "ungodly people". In 2 Peter (which many Bible scholars believe depended significantly on Jude's letter), Peter referred to these "godless men" as "false teachers". Paul referred to such men as "false apostles" (2 Corinthians 11:13) and "false brothers" (2 Corinthians 11:26; Galatians 2:4).

In all these cases, these men are referred to with the word "false" because the teachings they were spreading distorted or negated the gospel of Jesus Christ. For this reason, in the following chapters of this book, we will refer to such teaching as "false teaching". We will also refer to such teachers as "false teachers".

One common false teaching that impacts many churches in Africa today is *the prosperity doctrine*. Many people mistakenly refer to the *prosperity doctrine* as the *prosperity gospel*. A *doctrine* is a set of beliefs taught and held by a group of people. The prosperity teaching is a *doctrine*. It is not the *gospel*. There is only one gospel, and it is not primarily a doctrine about our material prosperity of health and wealth. Instead, it is principally the amazing news of our redemption from sin and spiritual separation from God, and about our spiritual transformation to become conformed to the image and likeness of Christ.

This teaching which seriously distorts the gospel goes by many names such as the word-of-faith, health-and-wealth, positive confession, and the name-it-and-claim-it doctrine.[3] It teaches that God always intends a trouble-free life for all Christians, characterized by perfect physical health and material prosperity.[4] The doctrine holds that because God desires financial prosperity for every one of his children, for a Christian to be in poverty is to lack faith and to be outside God's intended will.

Another false teaching we find in many of our churches is *religious legalism*. This view has been a thorn in the church's side ever since it started. It is the view that strictly observing religious laws is the basis for a relationship with God. In other words, our salvation or our status in God's sight depends on our efforts to do good things for God.

In the first story above, the preacher's theology is partially influenced by Gnosticism, a heretical teaching that severely troubled the church in the first-century world of Jude. Gnosticism will be more fully explained in the subsequent chapters of this book. In the second story above, the preacher's theology is influenced by the prosperity doctrine and religious legalism, which are both quite common in many of our churches in Africa today. Throughout this book, we will contrast these teachings with the gospel of Christ.

Over the years, I wondered repeatedly how we could address this situation. I interviewed many pastors in new and old churches alike, visiting their services, and comparing their teachings and practices with the gospel of Jesus Christ found in the New Testament (NT). In some churches, the departures from the gospel of Jesus Christ were very clear. In others, it wasn't so clear. In both cases, however, it was clear to me that African church members were not being taught the liberating content and implications of the real gospel of Christ Jesus.

Jude's Response

For many years, I agonized as I saw the church in Africa departing from the gospel of Jesus Christ. This burden repeatedly led me back to the Bible.

I was struck by Jude's response to false teaching in his day. His letter is one of the shortest books in the Bible, comprising only 25 verses, with considerably fewer than 1,000 words in the original Greek text. It doesn't even have chapter numbers because there is only one chapter. Yet, Jude's brief epistle is probably the strongest and the most direct rejection of teaching that departs from the gospel in the NT.[5] Jude was a leader in the early church, the brother of James (Jude 1), who probably came to faith after his half-brother, Christ Jesus, was resurrected from the dead (Acts 1:14; 1 Corinthians 9:5).

Jude's message is as relevant to the church today as when he first wrote his letter.

Jude wrote to a first-century Christian congregation around AD 65. This church was dealing with the Gnostic-influenced teaching described in the first story that features the two itinerant teachers in the Syrian Antioch church. Jude described these teachers as "ungodly people, who pervert the grace of our God into a licence for immorality and deny Jesus Christ our only Sovereign and Lord" (Jude 4). Jude urges his readers to "defend the faith that God has entrusted once for all time to his holy people" (verse 3 NLT) by rejecting any teaching that departs from the gospel.

I studied the original Greek text of the epistle for my doctorate. As I saw the similarities between Jude's time and our own, I realized that Jude's message is as relevant to the church today as it was when he first wrote his letter. I discovered precious nuggets that can help us to move from our serious theological crisis to a place of hope, truth, and power.

Jude wrote the letter to call upon his readers to reject every attempt to turn them away from the gospel of Jesus Christ. He boldly called them to allow the content and the implications of the gospel to shape every area of their lives. The content of the gospel is unavoidably linked with its implications of godly living and faithfulness to God.

For Jude, this requires Christians to contend for the gospel, affirm their faith, and live the right way. Jude emphasizes for all generations what a serious threat false teaching poses to genuine Christian faith and holy living.

In this book, we will examine Jude's message in the light of the whole NT gospel message by reviewing Jude's appeal to his original readers and then comparing it with our own context today. Each chapter will weave explanations and stories of the two contexts throughout, demonstrating the striking resemblance between the two. Each chapter will give us insights into our current situation and propose how Jude's message can help us to return to the gospel. At the end of each chapter, questions are provided to help you or your small Bible study group to prayerfully reflect on how the chapter relates to and applies to your context.

Throughout the book, I will offer my own experiences of living out the content and implications of the gospel in my walk with God. I hope this will show that the gospel message is not mere impractical theology. It is the amazing news of how God truly reconciles us to himself and enables us to practically experience the life of Christ in our daily lives today.

I pray this book serves as a clarion call for anyone who has strayed from the gospel to return to the truth. I want to offer you helpful guidelines for returning. If you remain faithful and seek to defend the gospel faith once and for all entrusted to God's holy people, I want to encourage you.

I pray that you will understand and live out the gospel of Jesus Christ in every area of your life. I pray that our churches in Africa that are growing numerically will also grow spiritually. May we truly become God's salt and light to transform our hurting communities and countries.

Finally, I pray that this book's call will go beyond Africa to the worldwide church of Jesus Christ. I pray it will challenge and bless the many Christians around the world facing similar challenges in their contexts today.

Questions for Reflection and Discussion

1. What drew you to this book? What are you hoping to learn from it?

2. Is there a person or a group you could invite to read and discuss this book with you?

3. Read through the book of Jude, nearly at the end of your Bible, just before Revelation. Write down a list of questions that you hope to answer as we go through Jude together.

CHAPTER 1

IDENTITY

Jude, a servant of Jesus Christ and a brother of James,
To those who have been called, who are loved in God
the Father and kept for Jesus Christ: Mercy, peace
and love be yours in abundance (Jude 1-2).

The Leader's Identity

Who was Jude? He introduces himself as the brother of James. He isn't talking about James the son of Zebedee and the brother of John, who was one of Jesus's closest disciples. Herod had executed that James very soon after Jesus's resurrection (Acts 12:2). Jude was referring to James, the brother of Jesus. After Jesus's ascension, his mother, Mary, and his brothers met with the disciples regularly in Jerusalem as they waited for Pentecost (Acts 1:14). Jesus's brother James became the general overseer of the Jerusalem church, playing an important role in the Jerusalem council's decision to accept Gentile believers (12:17; 15:13, 19-21, 31; 21:18). James was seen as a leader alongside Peter and John (Galatians 1:19; 2:9). He is also the one who wrote the book of James. In other words, Jude was not just the brother of one of the most powerful leaders of the early NT church; he was the brother of Christ Jesus himself.

How would any of our church leaders today with Jude's level of credentials identify or introduce themselves?

In several churches I visited during my doctoral research, I noticed lengthy admiring introductions of church leaders. These introductions included high-sounding ecclesiastical titles such as "Bishop", "Archbishop", "Apostle", and "Prophet." Often, these leaders had pursued honorary academic degrees to add to their titles. If there was anyone with a high public profile, they would quickly associate themselves with that person. For instance, they publicly kept company with politicians of questionable integrity, appearing regularly on popular TV and radio talk shows to discuss politics and recount stories of their rise to riches.

> How would any of our church leaders today with Jude's level of credentials identify or introduce themselves?

Often, after the church leader was introduced, I would see him enter the church service with a flourish. The congregation would applaud loudly. Minders and bodyguards would escort him to a specially built seat at the front of the church. The accompanying minders would then bow before the leader and retreat with bowed heads.

What a contrast to the way Jude introduces himself. He doesn't even claim to be the brother of Jesus. He humbly calls himself a slave of the Lord (Jude 1), one called to serve the Lord. Jude's identity was not primarily based on his family relationship with the Lord, but rather on his call to serve the Lord and his people.

Jesus taught that church leaders should be servants. He described himself in this way: "I am among you as one who serves" (Luke 22:27) and "The Son of Man did not come to be served, but to serve, and to give his life as a ransom for many" (Matthew 20:28; Mark 10:45). Christ left his glorious throne in heaven to come to earth. He humbled and sacrificed himself to die on a cross (John 13:1; Philippians 2:5-8).

Jesus said we should be servants, like him. Just before he lay down his life for us on the cross, Christ did a chore that only lowly servants in that culture at that time would do: washing the feet of his disciples (John 13:1-17). Then he said, "Now that I, your Lord and Teacher, have washed your feet, you also should wash one another's feet. I have set you an example that you should do as I have done for you" (13:14-15). Christ modelled weakness and service as the only acceptable way of all Christian leadership.

Jude followed the example of Jesus, defining himself as a servant of Christ rather than a prominent leader. We see church leaders today who tout themselves as being specially anointed "men of God" on whom we need to depend to receive God's blessing. By doing so, they ask us to make them our idols. The false teachers, who "boast about themselves" offer a sharp contrast with Jude's humility (Jude 16).

THE IMPLICATIONS

Does this mean that church leaders today should not call themselves Apostle or Prophet? First, I believe the trend of using these titles demonstrates a lack of understanding of the real meaning of these titles in the Bible. For example, the word *apostle* comes from the Greek word that means to send someone on a special mission as a messenger and personal representative of the one who sends him. In the NT this title was used for Christ himself (Hebrews 3:1), and it was used for the 12 disciples of Christ (Matthew 10:2). Being an apostle wasn't really about having authority, but about being a missionary spreading a message.

> The false teachers, who "boast about themselves" offer a sharp contrast with Jude's humility (Jude 16).

In the NT, *prophets* were believers who spoke under the direct inspiration of the Holy Spirit. They proclaimed and interpreted the gospel. They warned, exhorted, comforted, and edified the church so that it would grow to maturity (1 Corinthians 12:10; 14:3). Today, we see that church leaders do not receive this title from others because they are known for doing these things; instead, they add the title to their names and expect people to treat them with deference.

The underlying question, though, is why people claim these titles for themselves. These titles seem to give people authority over others. "Prophet" suggests that the leader has a special ability to hear from God. "Apostle" suggests a special calling and anointing to justify one's leadership. These titles suggest that the church leader is closer to God but more distant from the ordinary person. The impression these titles create is that people need these leaders to go to God on their behalf, to pray for them, to bless them, to interpret God's Word for them. In return, the people will gratefully respect, submit, and defer to these leaders.

Some people might respond that our cultures have traditionally always responded to leaders with unquestioning deference. Is it wrong for congregants to call leaders by these titles out of respect? Wouldn't it be rude to do otherwise? In Romans 13:7 the apostle Paul called upon his readers to give honour to those who deserve honour. This apostolic counsel, however, does not endorse treating leaders as demigods.

My main concern is with the leaders who demand this special treatment. How would they respond if they were not greeted with all their titles? If they would feel angry or offended, you can tell that their identity is not in being a servant of Christ. I observed one church founder who strongly emphasized loyalty to him personally. This church leader rails against any contrary opinion expressed by his subordinates, and calls them "traitors, villains, anarchists, mutineers, rebels, betrayers."[6]

People whose identity is truly in being a servant should actually feel uncomfortable when people honour them too much. They should try to discourage people from responding to them that way. They should be concerned when people praise them and should direct them to praise God instead. Consider what happened to Herod in Acts 12:21-23:

> On the appointed day Herod, wearing his royal robes, sat on
> his throne and delivered a public address to the people. They
> shouted, "This is the voice of a god, not of a man." Immediately,
> because Herod did not give praise to God, an angel of the Lord
> struck him down, and he was eaten by worms and died.

The first time I saw bodyguards and minders bow before the leader and walk away with bowed heads, I remembered when the apostle John fell down to worship at the feet of an angel who had been showing him stirring revelations of the last things (Revelation 22:8-9). But the angel said to the apostle, "Don't do that! I am a fellow servant with you and with your fellow prophets and with all who keep the words of this scroll. Worship God!" (22:9). It struck me that if even an angel was not to be worshipped in place of God, how much truer is this of human beings! In our church gatherings, only the ascended and glorified Christ, God the Son, is to be exalted and worshipped, not our church leaders.

Our church leaders deserve honour, but not in the form of exalting them above Christ.

Our church leaders deserve honour, but not in the form of exalting them above Christ. Church leaders must put aside the cultural prerogatives of superiority and privilege that prevail in their contexts. They should follow Christ's example by taking "the very nature" of servants who serve Christ and his people in godly humility, faith, and obedience to God. This would proclaim that Christ alone is exalted in his church and that they are just his servants.

The Readers' Identity

As he set out to address the urgent problem of false teaching that had crept into the church that he wrote to, Jude began by reminding his readers about who they were, and whose they were. He assured his readers that they were called, loved, and kept by God. This reminder gave them the inner confidence they needed to resist the errant teachers who had come into their church.

People in this church likely came from harsh socio-economic backgrounds. When Paul wrote to the Corinthian church, he mentioned that the early church was full of people who were not "wise by human standards; not many were influential; not many were of noble birth" (1 Corinthians 1:26). Ordinary Christians from humble backgrounds in the church that Jude wrote to may have felt insecure because of their low social status. The letter doesn't give us details, but it says that the false teachers "flatter others for their own advantage" (Jude 16). I imagine that would have been easy for false teachers to take advantage of the church members' humble backgrounds. Perhaps they would promise church members a good life of pleasure instead of trouble, a change in social status, or special spiritual revelations that gave them a sense of power.

In Africa today, pervasive unemployment, financial hardship, and poverty are sad realities of life for many people. Many young people have desperately tried to escape to Europe in search of greener pastures, even at the risk of dying in the Sahara Desert, Libya, and the Mediterranean Sea. Our countries are saddled with international debts despite their vast mineral wealth and great economic potential. We know all about ineffective educational systems, weak healthcare systems, poor infrastructure, endemic corruption in government, and economic mismanagement. Many people struggle with economic hardship, despair, and desperation. These harsh realities thus make many churchgoers very susceptible to flattery and false hope from false teachers, just as in the case of Jude's readers.

Amid these pressures, Jude reminded his readers that their Christian identity was rooted in the very gospel that these men were falsifying. Jude reassures them, and us, that our security does not come from our wealth or material possessions, but from God, who has called us, has loved us, and has promised to keep us for all eternity.

Do you remember when God called you? I do. I grew up in a Christian family and played a prominent role in my high school's Scripture Union. After high school, I moved to America to go to college. There, I backslid, adopted a loose lifestyle, and decided all religions were different roads to one grand, distant, undefined goal. Many years later as a young businessman, every penny that came into my life and business seemed to filter through my hands like a sieve.

A pastor from my youth counselled me to go off on a retreat to fast and pray. At the retreat venue, I settled down in the cottage to read a book I had borrowed from the pastor's library. The book, by Sir Norman Anderson, presented a Christian approach to other religions.[7] It explained how if it had been possible for God to deal with sin in any other way, God would certainly have spared his own Son the agony of dying on the cross. In a flash, my confused thinking about the equal merits of all religions fell away. I saw Christ on the cross and my utter sinfulness before God. I found myself falling to my knees. Deeply sorrowful and repentant, I confessed my sins to God and asked for his forgiveness. After a long time on my knees, I finally fell asleep. A heavy burden

> Our security does not come from our wealth or material possessions, but from God

had been lifted off my heart. That unforgettable call by God changed my life from that moment on.

God has called us "out of darkness into his marvellous light" in Christ (1 Peter 2:9 KJV). God in heaven has called us, ultimately, to heaven. He invites us to respond in faith and repentance to become part of his people, his divine family.

Jude declares that his readers are loved. Picture a mother, who loves her baby even though the baby's behaviour is not very lovable. The mother may have nearly died to birth the baby, the baby gives her sleepless nights, the baby smells, cries, and generally makes her life difficult. Even more than a mother, God loves us just because we are his children (Isaiah 49:15). The loving union of the Trinity created us, and we bear God's image.

So, God does not look at us and say, "I love you *because* you are good or holy or beautiful or righteous, because you read your Bible three times a day, or because you tithe regularly in your church." God's love accepts us just as we are. There is nothing that we can do to earn God's love – not how bad or good we have been, nor our promises to God to be better. God's love does not depend on us. It depends on his unchanging nature.

So, if preachers tell us we need to work hard to make God accept us, we know that's not true. We don't need to go looking for affirmation or value elsewhere when we know that we are already deeply loved by God.

Finally, Jude reminds his readers that they were being kept for Christ Jesus. Jude was concerned that his readers be kept safe from the influence of the men who had infiltrated their ranks with teaching that distorted the gospel. He reassured them that God the Father was keeping them safe from the evil one (1 John 5:18), for Christ's second coming (1 Corinthians 1:8; 1 Thessalonians 5:23), and for a wonderful future in the eternal Kingdom he will establish in this world upon Christ's return.

Preachers can easily use fear to influence people: the fear of witchcraft, the fear of demons, and the fear of the future. But Jude speaks to these anxious hearts: God will ensure that he meets our needs and that he keeps a firm hold of us to the very end of our days. We are important and precious to God. We have real hope for our future, regardless of our circumstances, our social status, or our material possessions. Our hope is based on God's faithfulness and unfailing promises.

We can draw encouragement from Jude's reminder of who we are and whose we are. God has called us, he loves us unconditionally, and he has promised to keep us through thick and thin in this world.

> He meets our needs and keeps a firm hold of us to the very end of our days. We are important and precious to God.

Lessons from History

These assurances Jude gave to his readers were very needed in the church in Ghana at the time that many of the currently fast-growing churches were founded in the mid- to late-1970s. If we look at our history, we can see how, at that time, the lack of these reassurances made people susceptible to those people who claimed special religious status as "the man of God".

Christianity first arrived in the Gold Coast (as Ghana was known then) through the ultimately unsuccessful proselytizing efforts of Portuguese Roman Catholic missionaries in the 15th century. By the mid-1800s, however, European Protestant missionaries had firmly established mission Christianity in the Gold Coast. By the beginning of the 20th century, mission Christianity and colonial influences had considerably modernized the Gold Coast through the introduction of Western education and medicine, the building of modern roads and railroads, the introduction of a cash economy, and the setting up of the British colonial civil service in the country. Many Africans at that time viewed the Christian faith with suspicion, seeing it as part of the colonial enterprise.[8]

As missionaries brought schools, hospitals, and liturgical churches to help Africans become Christians, they also introduced their Western worldview and culture. Many Africans who came into the church were alienated from their culture. They would have benefitted from Jude's message that they were called and loved by God just as they were, that Christ connected with and transformed their own culture. The missionaries' version of the gospel message did not adequately address their fears of malevolent spirits which was a huge concern in their worldviews from African Traditional Religions (ATR). They didn't feel the security that Jude describes of Christians being kept safe for Christ.

For this reason, the Africans failed to fully incorporate the implications of the gospel into their daily lives. They had an intellectual knowledge of the Bible and the Christian catechism, but it felt irrelevant to their worldview and their daily lives. The Christianity that took root in the country was largely nominal and left a spiritual void in the religious experience of the Africans.

Over time African prophets emerged from the ranks of the mission churches to fill this void. These prophets understood and related more readily to their people's felt religious needs. Their contextualized interpretations of the Bible resulted in Africanized preaching and teaching. Africans quickly accepted these prophets as specially anointed men of God. The three most prominent prophets in the Gold Coast at that time were William Wade Harris, John Swatson, and Sampson Oppong.[9]

From the popular ministries of these prophets arose the African Initiated Churches (AICs) that came to be known as "spiritual churches." The AIC churches were popular for several reasons. First, aspiring African clergy had experienced racism in the white-led mission churches. Once again, they hadn't been treated as if they were called and loved by God. AICs also took seriously the ATR worldview that blamed evil spirits for sickness and other woes. These African prophets addressed such concerns with faith healing and exorcisms. They emphasized spiritual gifts and offered practical solutions to the problems of African daily life. Their AIC churches gave an important place to vernacular Bibles, local African languages and liturgies, supernatural healing, and revelations through prophecy, trances, and dreams. In many AIC churches, the religious experience was indigenous, exciting, spontaneous, and unrestricted, which gave a sense of freedom from foreign domination.[10]

When I was growing up in Ghana in the 1960s, my mother was an ardent member of an AIC church. She faithfully took her children to this AIC church every Sunday. I remember the services being long and lively, with boisterous singing, dancing, and testimonies of what God had done in the lives of the church members, such as providing them with miraculous healing, jobs, and successful businesses. The church founders were revered; every word they spoke was seen as coming directly from God. My mother shared with us some of the prophecies of the church leaders that had come true in her life. This included the healing of her mother (my grandmother), who had been riddled with sickness for many years and whom medical treatment had failed to help.

We can celebrate the fact that these prophets challenged nominalism in the mission churches, calling the church to prayer and the gifts of the Holy Spirit. Many of their Spirit-led contributions to the growth of the church in Ghana are positive historical realities that we should thank God for. For

> We should thank God for many of the African prophets' contributions to the church.

instance, they showed that the power of Christ the gospel brings into our lives can adequately answer our questions and needs as Africans.

However, the AICs' rejection of nominal liturgical Christianity laid the groundwork for the unquestioning acceptance of locally raised church leaders in Ghana today as specially anointed men and women of God. The mission churches, many of which still exist today, kept formal structures that could hold leaders accountable. The prophets and AICs had split away from mission churches, so they often left those accountability structures behind. The later prophetic Pentecostal phenomenon also emphasized that the Holy Spirit's power is all that is needed to justify someone's ministry. Without denominational structures, boards of elders, or requirements for theological training, most of the power to manage the church and direct the teaching rested with the prophet or founder.

Today, the founders of many new, fast-growing churches have near-total control and autonomy over all church management and financial decisions. These church founders are regarded and treated as being infallible "men of God." Social scientist Paul Gifford notes that "many of these new churches have absolutely nothing except the pastor's vision."[11] Church members are so used to accepting the authority of these leaders that they don't question their teaching or practices, even when it contradicts the gospel.

> These church founders are regarded and treated as being infallible "men of God."

Exalting Christ

We can address this problem by following Jude's example. He knows that Christ is the real head of the church (Ephesians 5:23; Colossians 1:18), not himself or other leaders. So, he humbles himself as a servant of Christ and exalts Christ as Lord.

Right from the beginning, and all through his epistle, Jude reminds his readers that since Christ saved us through the cross, he must be our Lord. Jude describes Jesus as, "our only Sovereign and Lord" (verse 4) and "our Lord Jesus Christ" (verses 17 and 21). Jude ends his epistle with a reminder that, as the Lord of the church, Christ Jesus is the mediator between God and the faithful; it is through Christ that praise is offered to God.

We can respect our leaders, but only Jesus deserves worship. He is God. Thomas realized this when Jesus appeared to the disciples after his resurrection because he called Jesus, "My Lord and my God!" (John 20:28). Christ is enthroned in heaven. After his resurrection, Jesus ascended to heaven and sat at the right hand of the Father, crowned in glory (1 Peter 1:21, Hebrews 1:3; 2:9). God has exalted Christ to the highest place and given him the name that is above every name (Philippians 2:9).

Exalting Christ Today

So how do we honour or exalt Christ today? We obey his Word and, in the power of the Holy Spirit, try to live in a manner pleasing to him. Christ is *Immanuel*, which means God with us (Matthew 1:23). We honour Christ when we acknowledge him as the real leader of the church present among us whenever we gather as his people (Matthew 18:20).

In our church gatherings, we honour ourselves instead of Christ when we sing songs about ourselves that make us feel good about ourselves. We honour Christ when we sing songs and hymns that praise him with great devotion and reverence for what he has done for us on the cross. In one church I know, they do not have anyone

> We honour Christ when we acknowledge him as the real leader of the church present among us whenever we gather as his people (Matthew 18:20).

singing or playing instruments on stage because they want the singing to be focused, not on church musicians, but on exalting Christ.

When we laud our programmes and our denominational success as indications of our good planning, we honour ourselves. We honour Christ when we refer all our plans and programmes to him in prayer. This is what marked the early disciples as being the followers of Christ (Acts 4:13; 5:29).

When Jesus washed the disciples' feet, John 13:3-4 says, "Jesus knew that the Father had put all things under his power, and that he had come from God and was returning to God; so he got up from the meal, took off his outer clothing, and wrapped a towel around his waist." Jesus knew who he was, where he came from, and where he was going. Out of that security, he served God and the people of God.

The first two verses of Jude remind us of who we are. Because Jesus died for us, we can stand in the assurance that we are called into God's family, loved as God's children, and kept safe from evil. We can stand firm on this truth when false teachers try to flatter us.

Because we are secure in our identity as God's beloved children, we don't need to be like the false teachers, to boast about ourselves, seek honour, or prove we are somebody. Jesus showed us this when he washed the disciples' feet. Likewise, Jude didn't need to prove his worth by mentioning his credentials and connections. We are free to be servants of Christ, the one who is worthy of all honour, praise, and worship.

> We are called into God's family, loved as God's children, and kept safe from evil.

Questions for Reflection and Discussion

1. Can you imagine Jude visiting your church today? How do you think he would want to be introduced?

2. What do you think is the difference between a healthy respect for leaders and exalting them, instead of Christ? Can you describe some examples of each?

3. As you reflect on your identity in Christ as being called, loved, and kept, which of these speaks most to your heart?

Courage

CHAPTER 2
CONTEND FOR THE FAITH

Dear friends, although I was very eager to write to you
about the salvation we share, I felt compelled to write
and urge you to contend for the faith that was once
for all entrusted to God's holy people (Jude 3).

Jude had hoped to write to his readers about salvation generally, but the problem of false teachers infiltrating the church came to his attention. To him, this was so urgent that he had to address it directly. In the face of this threat, Jude wanted his readers to fight for "the faith that was once for all entrusted to God's holy people."

Every time the New Testament refers to *the* faith, it is a reference to the good news of the gospel of Jesus Christ (Philippians 1:25-27; 1 Timothy 4:6; 1 Corinthians 16:13; 2 Corinthians 13:5; Titus 1:4). Jude's readers would know that when he said "the salvation" and "the faith" he meant the gospel of Jesus Christ. However, in our churches today it is not always clear that we mean the same thing when we talk about the gospel. We hear this word *gospel* so often that we simply assume we understand it. We talk about *gospel* music or *the gospel truth*. The word *gospel* is a translation of a Greek word that means *good news*. But many churchgoing people, even church leaders, do not really understand what this good news is.

In 1 Corinthians 15:3-4, Paul summarizes the gospel he received when he was converted: "Christ died for our sins according to the Scriptures, . . . he was buried, [and] he was raised on the third day according to the Scriptures." Eyewitnesses still alive at the time Paul wrote could testify that Christ was really buried and rose from the dead. The Scriptures Paul refers to are OT prophecies about Christ dying for the sins of God's people and rising from the dead. For Paul, the heart of the gospel is the good news about the historically verifiable death and resurrection of Jesus Christ of Nazareth, 2,000 years ago in Palestine. Let's explore what this good news means for everyone.

> We hear this word *gospel* so often that we simply assume we understand it.

Religious Legalism

I recently attended a wedding at a church where all the people had to take off their shoes before climbing onto the platform where the pulpit was located. They saw this as a holy place and believed that their shoes would desecrate it. I was shocked because this reminded me of when the Old Testament priests had to clean themselves before entering God's presence. But through the gospel, we are cleansed by the blood of Christ and we can approach his throne anytime, anywhere, just as we are (Hebrews 4:16). The incident vividly illustrated to me how easy it is for us to fall back into the idea that we must clean ourselves and our sins before God can accept us. While it may not always be this visually obvious, this attitude of religious legalism is very common in many of our churches today.

Many people believe that their good behaviour makes God accept them. Have you ever been made to believe that if you want to be right with God, you need to obey the Ten Commandments, you need to go to church regularly, you need to pray, you need to read your Bible, and you need to pay your tithes faithfully to the church? Many of us have been taught that this is how we gain God's favour for our prayers and earn his blessing.

This mistaken understanding of the gospel is called *religious legalism*. It views the strict observance of religious laws as the basis for a relationship with God. Religious legalism mixes up the order of steps involved in becoming a Christian. It teaches that to be a good Christian, you believe in the Lord Jesus Christ. Second, you obey the Ten Commandments as best as you can. Only then will you be saved. But the gospel says that the moment you believe in the Lord Jesus Christ you are saved. The Holy Spirit comes to live in you and empowers you to obey God, not in order to receive God's salvation, but because you have received it already through your repentance and faith in Christ.

In Jesus's day, religious Jews mistakenly believed that strictly obeying the Law of Moses earned them God's acceptance and salvation. Jesus repeatedly taught that they had lost the original intention of the OT Law (see Mark 2:23–3:6; 7:9-13). This is because these Jews mixed up the order in how God had related with the people of Israel.

God delivered the Israelites from captivity in Egypt. He saved them and made them his people not because they deserved it, but because he loved them, chose them, and was a faithful God (Deuteronomy 7:7-9). God affirmed this in Isaiah 43:1: "I have redeemed you; I have summoned you by name; you are mine."

Many churchgoing people express a sense of fear and guilt whenever they miss going to church

After saving the Israelites and making them his people purely by his grace, God then gave the Israelites the Law. The Law's purpose was to show them how to live in a manner that would be a blessing to themselves and to demonstrate to their pagan neighbours what it looked like to be in a covenant relationship with God. Obeying the Law did not earn them God's favour, but it was to be a grateful response to God for the grace he had *already* extended to them.

Like the religious legalists of Jesus's time, when we seek to earn God's salvation and his blessing through what we do, we are trying to put God in our debt. When bad things happen to you, have you ever found yourself saying, "Why has this happened to me? I pray, I read my Bible, I pay my tithes!" Our false pride tells us God owes us something and that he is simply not living up to his end of the bargain. It is as if we want to be our own saviour through our efforts.

Yet we also fear our own efforts will fail us. We fear missing God's salvation and his blessing if we let up on our religious practices. Many churchgoing people express a sense of fear and guilt whenever they miss going to church for one reason or the other, when they fail to pray "enough", when they don't read their Bible "enough", or when they don't tithe "enough".

In reality, we can never do enough to save ourselves. God is completely holy and righteous, so our sins spiritually separate us from him and place us under his righteous judgement. To be delivered from this fate, we need to humbly admit that we need God to save us and forgive us.

Throughout the OT, the people of God had to sacrifice the blood of bulls and goats to atone for their sins. In Hebrews 10:4, however, we read that "it is impossible for the blood of bulls and goats to take away sins." It is human beings who have sinned against God, not the innocent bulls and goats. So, ultimately, it requires the blood of a human being to atone for the sins of human beings.

So, either we die for our sins ourselves, or we need to find someone to die for us. That person must have no sin of his own to die for and must be willing to die in our place. Only God himself has no sin. Only God can represent all of us since he is our Creator. And only God loves us enough to make such a sacrifice.

So, God became a real human being in the form of Christ Jesus so that the blood of a sinless human representative would be shed to permanently atone for our sins. "Christ also suffered for our sins, the righteous for the unrighteous, to bring [us] to God" (1 Peter 3:18). When Christ cried out on the cross, "My God, my God, why have you forsaken me?" he was announcing to all the world that he was taking upon himself our spiritual separation and alienation from God so that when we place our faith in him, we can now be reconciled to God (Matthew 27:46). This is good news about how and why God can forgive the sins of human beings so that we can be reconciled to him and become his spiritual sons and daughters.

Paul personally experienced the profound difference between religious legalism and the gospel. Before his conversion, he observed the Law in the strictest form of Judaism, even persecuting the church of God in his zeal (Philippians 3:4-10). Then the resurrected, ascended, and exalted Christ appeared to him. Paul testified in 1 Corinthians 15:9-10 that he didn't even deserve to be called an apostle, but God's grace in and through Christ had transformed him. His hard work did not make him acceptable to God, but his gratitude for what God's grace had done in his life empowered him to work harder in his ministry than even the rest of the apostles.

As Paul found, we no longer need to obey God out of the fear and anxiety of losing our salvation. Instead, we obey him out of joy and gratitude for what he has done for us and given to

By God's grace, we become his children who now have power over sin, and whose core identity is defined by what Christ has done for us.

us through Christ. The good news of the gospel is that all our praying, all our Bible reading, all our churchgoing, and all our giving are not religious works through which we make ourselves acceptable to God. Instead, these spiritual disciplines deepen our relationship with our heavenly Father and help us grow into spiritual maturity. By God's grace, we become his children who now have power over sin, and whose core identity is defined by what Christ has done for us.

Can you see how the gospel is the exact opposite of religious legalism? While religious legalism tells us to try to make ourselves acceptable to God, the gospel is the good news that tells us what God has done to make us acceptable to him. Christianity is not a set of rules for becoming right with God, but our relationship with God through Jesus Christ. The gospel announces *good news*; it does not just give *good advice* about reconciliation with God. The gospel does not exhort us to *do* something; it declares what has already been *done* for us in Christ.[12]

Freedom from Fear

Several years ago, when my father passed away, the funeral was conducted at the church in Ghana where he had been a church elder. As the firstborn in my family and an ordained minister, the church allowed me to preach in the memorial service on a Friday morning.

On Monday morning, the family met to review the expenses that had been incurred in laying my father's remains to rest. Traditionally, these functions include pouring libation to the ancestors. My uncle, who is also an elder in the Presbyterian church, hosted the function at his home. Before the ceremony began, the head of the family, my father's older cousin, turned to me and said: "Kwasi, we know that you are an ordained minister, you teach pastors in that Bible school in Kenya, and we all heard you preach the gospel on Friday. And we respect that. However, we have our own African theology, which we practised before the missionaries came to Africa, and we are going to practise it now." Completely ignoring my presence and the gospel message I had preached in the memorial service on Friday morning, they poured libation to the ancestors and went ahead with all the other pagan rites.

Here were church leaders, blatantly contradicting the gospel! Many African churchgoers, like my senior relatives, revert to traditional African religious norms when it comes to funerals, weddings, and many social gatherings because their leaders have not taught them the gospel nor modelled how to contend for it.

Like my relatives, many people's real beliefs and worldview are strongly influenced by African Traditional Religions (ATR).[13] In this worldview, the natural world of rocks, trees, mountains, rivers, etc. is inhabited by spirit beings that control every aspect of human life. People are afraid because they are subject to the whims of spirit beings, which can do them good or harm. Departed ancestors who have now gone into the realm of the supernatural can act as intermediaries in the spirit world. To meet one's needs, one must appease, manipulate, or seek the favour of these spirits. To achieve their objectives, those who hold to this worldview try to get supernatural knowledge and power through divination, witchcraft, sorcery, necromancy, astrology, prophecies, ancestors, omens, charms, and spells.

A gospel presentation that focuses on sin may not feel relevant to someone with this worldview. For instance, early Western missionaries to Africa emphasized deliverance from personal sin through repentance, similar to what we have said above about the problem of sin and religious legalism.

However, Africans were often more concerned about deliverance from the influence of evil powers in the unseen spiritual realm. This was what they felt affected their poverty, their health, crop failure, marital discord, infant mortality, and so on. Africans with this worldview often did not consider themselves sinners if they had lived according to societal customs. They had never killed anyone or stolen anything, so how could they be sinners deserving death? What did sin have to do with God?

In the Garden of Eden, our first parents believed Satan's lie that we can be equal to God. In some ways, this is what people influenced by ATR try to do when they seek to control the spiritual world. But humans cannot plan, direct, and control things on earth and in heaven.[14] The Bible teaches that God is sovereign and humans depend on him. In Jeremiah 10:23, for example, the prophet declares, "Lord, I know that people's lives are not their own; it is not for them to direct their steps."

Romans 1:25 explains that our first parents, and the rest of us ever since, "exchanged the truth of God for a lie, and worshipped and served created things, rather than the Creator". It only makes sense to people with an ATR worldview when they realize that they have offended God the Creator, that they have been worshipping and making sacrifices to the creation and other spirits, but that God the Creator alone is worthy of worship.

As a result of believing Satan's lie in the Garden, Ephesians 2:1-2 tells us that humans moved from God's Kingdom into the kingdom of Satan. There, Satan's power and authority dominate the worldview and the daily lives of those who live without reference to God and his will. Supernatural evil power keeps people who believe in ATR in fear, spiritual bondage, and spiritual darkness. "The god of this age has blinded the minds of unbelievers, so that they cannot see the light of the gospel of the glory of Christ" (2 Corinthians 4:4).

The ATR worldview believes that human beings must seek the favour of the spirits by making costly sacrifices and pouring libations to their dead ancestors. But the blood of animals could never appease the Creator. How could the animals make up for the sins of humans (Hebrews 10:4)? As we mentioned earlier, Hebrews explains,

> Since the children have flesh and blood, he too shared in their humanity so that by his death he might break the power of him who holds the power of death – that is, the devil – and free those who all their lives were held in slavery by their fear of death . . . For this reason he had to be made like them, fully human in every way, in order that he might become a merciful and faithful high priest in service to God, and that he might make atonement for the sins of the people (Hebrews 2:14-15, 17).

The powerful gospel truth is that Jesus Christ is the Christian's ultimate ancestor. Christ Jesus, God the Son, became a real human being we can relate to. He had no sins that needed sacrificing for, so when he died, his sacrifice appeased God's wrath towards us. Since he was God, his one-time sacrifice covered all people (Hebrews 9:25-28).

Unlike our dead ancestors, Christ rose from the dead. He is living, but unseen. Jesus conquered the power of death, the devil who holds the power of death, and the fear he holds over us. Christ is the mediator who intercedes for us in the spiritual realm (Hebrews 8:6). He is seated at the right hand of God on high. He is our true source of divine help and a life of spiritual abundance in this world (John 10:10; 14:13-14; 16:23-24). His unconditional love for us, permanently displayed on the cross, is the reason we should have faith in him alone.[15]

Many people do not understand this gospel truth, so they come into the church still feeling vulnerable,

> Christ's unconditional love for us is the reason we should have faith in him alone.

clutching the Bible in one hand and ATR in the other, just to hedge their bets. But the gospel of Christ alone offers God's power, the only true protection against the power of evil spirits. Deliverance only comes from God, the Creator. People need to replace their faith in ATR methods with faith in Jesus, who can deal with evil spiritual powers and meet all their needs.

Many churches in Africa have grown quickly because they speak to this fear. In one church service I attended, the pastor said, "There are many of you who would be very successful were it not for all the evil forces and witches in your family working against you!" This is a commonly held belief among those who still hold a strong ATR view. For this reason, in these churches, their deliverance sessions overemphasize the power of evil instead of reassuring people that Christ is more powerful. Our churches need to proclaim that we have been redeemed, forgiven, born again, and delivered from Satan's power by God's work through Christ,[16] as Jude affirms in the very first verse of his epistle.

Deliverance from Fear, Guilt, and Shame

We have discussed the gospel from two angles so far. The first angle focused on sin in terms of religious legalism and individual **guilt**. Western presentations of the gospel have often taken this approach. That gospel presentation is true and needed today because we are sinners and we easily fall prey to religious legalism. At the same time, if it is the only understanding of the gospel, African churchgoers still feel vulnerable to demonic forces, which the Bible affirms are real.

> Our churches need to proclaim that we have been redeemed, forgiven, born again, and delivered from Satan's power by God's work through Christ

On the other hand, presenting the gospel as deliverance from Satan and his demons feels very relevant to the **fear** that pervades an ATR worldview, and churches that preach this message in Africa grow quickly. However, many churches today go too far, saying that Satan is the cause of all suffering, and therefore the way to deal with sin is by being delivered from evil powers, neglecting the repentance from sin that Scripture calls for. Can we find a balance between these two aspects of the gospel message?

The church in Africa needs a balanced view of the gospel that incorporates both guilt and fear. If we look at the origin of sin during the Fall, we find that sin damaged our relationships with God, others, and ourselves, causing us to feel fear, shame, and guilt.[17] The gospel delivers us from these effects of sin that hobble our lives.

Fear fills our lives with a sense of insecurity about the future, the unknown, and death. We look to any available sources of power to protect us from evil and misfortune. Guilt is an individual feeling that we have done something wrong. Shame is a foreboding feeling about how others see us; that deep within, we are never good enough. We feel that if others really knew us, they would reject us. So, we seek status, beauty, and material success to cover up our sense of inadequacy.

These deep-seated feelings are our human legacy from when our first parents disobeyed God and ate from the forbidden tree of the knowledge of good and evil. Bible scholars call this *the Fall* because Adam and Eve *fell away* from God's original good plans for them and his creation. All of us, inside them, fell too. God had designed us for a perfect relationship with him. This perfect relationship with the all-powerful, loving creator of the world naturally precluded being afraid of God or of anything else.

But the serpent lied to our first parents, tempting Adam and Eve to rebel against God, to mistrust, disobey, and dishonour God by trying to become like God themselves (Genesis 3:4-5). Our first parents, with all of us inside them, believed the lie and broke away from God's rule and their relationship with him.

Before this, the man and his wife were both naked and they were not ashamed (Genesis 2:25). Afterwards, our first parents sewed fig leaves to cover their shame (Genesis 3:7). Before the Fall, we knew God's perfect love for us, God's goodness, and his loving control of our lives and all our circumstances. But fear and guilt about their disobedience had erased our first parents' sense of God's love for them. Now they felt rejection and failure.

When God came looking for Adam and Eve, they hid because they were afraid (Genesis 3:8-9). Without God's protection, we feel vulnerable to evil forces, unpredictable circumstances, the future, and death. So, we seek power to influence the world, whether that power comes from powerful people, religious specialists, or rituals that promise to help us.

A good example of how little control we have over our lives is the COVID-19 pandemic. This pandemic has wreaked havoc, caused illness, and severely affected every economy in the world. We have lost countless lives, businesses, and livelihoods. The pandemic has left in its wake ruined lives, scarred bodies, bereaved families, and devastated communities. And yet, modern man, with all his scientific knowledge, failed to foresee this pandemic, belying the fallacy of our human claims of being able to predict, command, and control our destiny.

Immediately after Adam and Eve's sin, God pronounced this judgement upon the snake, Satan: "And I will put enmity between you and the woman, and between your offspring and hers; he will crush your head, and you will strike his heel" (Genesis 3:15). This meant that one day a man would come out of a woman – Jesus, born of the virgin Mary. He would destroy Satan's control over humans and restore us back to God's original good purposes for his creation.

. . . our human claims of being able to predict, command, and control our destiny are a fallacy.

As 1 John 3:8-9 says, "The reason the Son of God appeared was to destroy the devil's work."

The good news is that, on the cross, Christ took upon himself the guilt and shame of our sin. When we put our faith in what he did for us on the cross, we can stand before God, free from guilt and shame (Romans 8:1; 10:11; Hebrews 10:22). Fear has to do with punishment for sin, but God's love displayed by Christ on the cross casts out our fear (1 John 4:18). If the omnipotent Son of God suffered torture and even death for us, we can trust him.[18] As the psalmist wrote, "When I am afraid, I put my trust in you" (Psalm 56:3). We can trust that he is in control of this world with his wisdom, his power, and his love for us. And that trust removes our fear, our shame, and our guilt. It gives us a relationship with the Father, his power, and his eternal life.

Equipping churches in Africa to understand how the gospel addresses fear, guilt, and shame can enable us to take a balanced approach to sin and demons, our individual relationship with God, and our relationship with others.

We can stand before God, free from guilt and shame.

Contending for the Gospel

Jude 3 says: "I felt compelled to write and urge you to contend for the faith that was once for all entrusted to God's holy people." We have explained that what Jude meant by "the faith" was the gospel. Now, what did he mean by *contending* for the faith? The word *contending* in Jude's day was used for athletes who competed in the Greek Olympic Games, much as we have Olympic contenders today who strive, with everything they have, to win.[19]

The word *entrusted* reminded Jude's readers that the apostles themselves had given them the responsibility to ensure that the truth of the gospel stayed pure. They had to guard against any change or contamination in what had been given to them. In the face of false teaching, you and I are responsible as Christians to know and defend the gospel as presented to us in the NT.

To Jude and the other church leaders of his day, it was clear that the authenticity of the gospel was at stake, and that it is worth fighting for. Paul was "not ashamed of the gospel, because it is the power of

In the face of false teaching, you and I are responsible as Christians to know and defend the gospel.

God that brings salvation to everyone who believes" (Romans 1:16). He warned his readers that any teaching that departed from the gospel of Jesus Christ that he had shared with them was no gospel at all; even if an angel from heaven preached another gospel, God would curse that angel (Galatians 1:6-8)!

Jude's readers needed to contend, to defend, to fight for this gospel truth. I recently observed an altercation between an employee and one of the directors of a certain company. The police asked me to write a statement. I could contend for, or stand by, my written statement because I was a first-hand witness. Jude and his readers could contend for the gospel because they had first-hand experience of God's salvation through the gospel of Jesus Christ.

The apostles were first-hand witnesses of Jesus's resurrection. They spent 40 days with the resurrected Christ before his ascension. He taught them the gospel implications of his life, death, and resurrection (Luke 24:37-53; Acts 1:1-11) and instructed them to be his witnesses to the ends of the earth.

Confucius, the founder of Confucianism, is long dead and buried. Today, we can visit his grave in China. Buddha, the founder of the Buddhist faith, is also long dead and buried. Today, we can visit his grave in India. Mohammed, the founder of the Islamic faith, is long dead and buried. Millions of Muslims faithfully visit his grave in Mecca every year. But Jesus Christ is alive today! His empty grave proves the gospel is true: he really did save us on the cross and rise again from the dead!

The gospel so transformed the apostles that, according to church tradition, all but one of them died as martyrs contending for the gospel. For instance:

- Jude was martyred with an axe in Beirut, together with the apostle Simon the Zealot (AD 65).
- James, the brother of Jude, was thrown down from the pinnacle of the Temple in Jerusalem and beaten to death with a club (AD 69).
- The apostle Paul was condemned to death by decapitation in Rome by Emperor Nero (AD 64).
- The apostle Peter was crucified head down (AD 64), saying he was unworthy to be crucified in the same manner as Christ.

Jude's call to contend for the gospel is just as relevant today as it was in the early church. In fact, we have African examples of people who have striven, with everything they have, for the gospel.

In the 1970s, the church in Uganda faced severe persecution at the hands of Idi Amin's Muslim soldiers. One evening, soldiers stormed a church meeting in the capital, Kampala. Many of the churchgoers escaped from the clutches of the soldiers by claiming that they were not members of the church; they had only come to pick up their relatives. The pastor of the church and his wife, who are friends of mine, were among those arrested. They were imprisoned and tortured for many months, but they refused to recant their faith. By God's mercy, they were eventually released and fled to Kenya.

> The gospel so transformed the apostles that, all but one of them died as martyrs contending for the gospel.

Another example is Byang Kato, the late "Founding Father of African Evangelical Theology".[20] A generation ago, he took up Jude's call to contend for the faith. Kato's father belonged to the fetish priest family of his tribe. A few months after Kato's birth in Kaduna State, Nigeria in 1936, his father proudly dedicated him to carrying on the family tradition as a fetish priest. Of the seven children born after Kato, only one lived. In the ATR worldview, Kato's survival confirmed that the power of Kuno, the devil, was looking after him.

Christian missionaries had started a school near their town and young Kato pleaded with his parents for over a year to go to the school. Finally, at the age of 12, Kato started school, going in the afternoons after working with his father in the mornings.

One day, his Nigerian teacher explained the way of salvation, using the story of Noah and the ark. That day, standing before the class, Kato prayed to receive God's free gift of salvation in Jesus Christ. When his father learned of Kato's public commitment, he beat him, refused to give him food, and took his shirt away.[21] Kato learned early on to contend for the gospel.

Kato was discipled by missionaries and defied convention by gaining a Doctor of Theology from Dallas Theological Seminary in the early 1970s. He was the first African to be appointed the General Secretary of the Association of Evangelicals of Africa and Madagascar, now the Association of Evangelicals of Africa (AEA).

While contemporary African scholars advocated embracing ATR concepts to recover African culture, Kato boldly declared that these ideas contradicted the gospel of Jesus Christ.[22] He supported making the gospel culturally relevant, such as by using local languages, songs, and concepts, without compromising it.[23] Only in Christ, he contended, could Africans find their true identity as Christian Africans.[24]

Kato cast a vision for establishing two evangelical Bible schools in West and East Africa, an African evangelical theological journal, and an accrediting agency that sets standards of evangelical theological education in Africa. Today, all these dreams have been realized. Although he passed away when he was only 39, Byang Kato's legacy of contending for the faith lives on and inspires us today.

> Only in Christ, Byang Kato contended, could Africans find their true identity as Christian Africans.

We share the same salvation as Jude and his readers, the same salvation as the Ugandan believers and Byang Kato. The amazing news is that Christ has redeemed us from sin and spiritual separation from God. That gospel sets us free from religious legalism and the kingdom of Satan. It takes away our guilt, shame, and fear. It reassures us that God is remaking us into the image and likeness of Christ. Jude saw the redemptive, life-changing importance of the gospel. It was worth everything to contend for it. The witnesses of the Resurrection entrusted it to Jude's readers and to us. It is our solemn duty to safeguard it from being watered down or changed in any way.

The last paragraph of Kato's book, *Theological Pitfalls in Africa*, charges us to take up this call just as Jude charges his readers:

> Following in the footsteps of the New Testament church, Christians in Africa should be prepared to say, "For me to live is Christ, and to die is gain (Phil. 1:21)." Africa needs her Polycarps, Athanasiuses, and Martin Luthers, ready to *contend for the faith at all costs*. The Lord of the church who has commanded Bible-believing Christians to *contend earnestly for the faith (Jude 3)*, has also said, "Yes, I am coming quickly" (Rev. 22:20). May we give the reverberating response, "Amen, Come Lord Jesus"[25] (emphasis added).

Questions for Reflection and Discussion

1. What are some ways that you have tried to earn God's favour through your religious activities such as going to church, giving tithes and offerings, etc.?

2. How does our perspective of God change when we do good deeds out of gratitude for what God's grace has done instead of doing good deeds as an attempt to earn his favour?

3. Can you think of situations where people clutch the Bible in one hand and ATR in their other hand?

4. What do you think about the idea that the gospel offers us freedom from fear, guilt, and shame?

5. What did you learn from Byang Kato's story?

CHAPTER 3

SECRETLY SLIPPED IN

*For certain individuals whose condemnation was written
about long ago have secretly slipped in among you. They are
ungodly people, who pervert the grace of our God into
a licence for immorality and deny Jesus Christ
our only Sovereign and Lord (Jude 4).*

In verse 4, Jude describes these individuals with their errant
teaching as having "secretly slipped" into the church. The Greek
word Jude used also means "to infiltrate." Peter and Paul used the
same word to describe false teachers and heretical teachings they
were combatting in their letters (2 Peter 2:1; Galatians 2:4). Like
these individuals in Jude who had infiltrated the church with
teaching that contradicted the gospel, much false teaching has today
infiltrated the church in Africa. Let's trace the history to find where
this teaching came from and how it slipped into our churches. I will
use the case study of Ghana, my home country, to illustrate.

The Case of Ghana

In many African countries, including Ghana, the replacement of

> Like these individuals in Jude who had infiltrated the church with teaching that contradicted the gospel, much false teaching has today infiltrated the church in Africa.

the gospel with teaching that differs from the gospel in many of the new growing churches has its historical roots in the socio-economic realities that prevailed in the country at the time these churches were founded.

In 1957, the Convention People's Party (CPP) and its charismatic leader, Kwame Nkrumah, agitated for and negotiated independence for the Gold Coast from the British. In the years following the country's independence, Nkrumah's government was bedevilled by corruption, nepotism, economic mismanagement, and political oppression. As his rule became more dictatorial and intolerant of opposition, Nkrumah took on the title of *Osagyefo*. This is an Akan word that roughly translates as "Saviour" or "National Deliverer." As a boy, I remember that we had to sing choruses in primary school daily in his praise. One ditty I still clearly recall, had the line, "Nkrumah never dies, never dies, never dies . . ."

THE 1966 COUP

Nkrumah's rule was ended by a popular military *coup d'état* when I was 10 years old. My family lived a stone's throw away from Flagstaff House, the official home and office complex of the president. In the early hours of January 24th, 1966, the sound of gunshots woke us up. Soldiers barked "Stop or I shoot!" to motorists driving past Flagstaff House on the street outside our home.

My father was away in Nigeria on an official trip. My mother herded all of us into our parents' bedroom and under their bed. The bullets from the guns of the soldiers tore through the mosquito netting on the windows of our apartment, loudly shattered the glass louvres, and tore the window curtains into shreds. My mother kept those torn curtains for many years as a memento of how her family, by the grace of God, survived that military coup. For many years after this, these frightening sounds haunted me in nightmares.

The coup-making soldiers attacked Flagstaff House to dislodge the government soldiers who had evidently been taken by surprise. I remember that in the early afternoon of that fateful day, an uneasy calm began to settle over the neighbourhood. My mother made a furtive foray outside the apartment. Miraculously, she ran into her cousin, who was a senior military officer in the army. He quickly organized for us to be evacuated from our home, to find shelter in another uncle's home in a different part of the city. The following Sunday, my mother went forward in our AIC church to testify how God had so faithfully saved her family.

To this day, I remember the scenes of jubilation across the country that greeted the 1966 military coup. Kwame Nkrumah's statue, with his arm raised in a victory salute that had stood on the grounds of the Ghana Parliament for many years, was smashed and toppled, a telling symbol of the end of his misrule. As dazed and emaciated men and women were released from prison after years of political detention without trial, their relatives received them with tears of relief and rejoicing.

Ghanaians were disillusioned and just plain tired of the many years of Kwame Nkrumah's misrule that had resulted in empty store shelves and a complete lack of freedom of expression. We expected that the end of Kwame Nkrumah's ill-fated rule would usher in more prosperous days.

PRAYER AND EMERGING CHURCH LEADERS

Sadly, the next 15 years were full of political instability as a succession of military and civilian governments suspended the constitution and banned political parties. This led to a severe economic decline and harsh living conditions for most Ghanaians. As successive governments could not address the worsening problems, Christians began to view their hardships as God's judgement on the nation, particularly on the government and business elite who were getting rich at the expense of the starving masses. Both the mission churches and the AICs began to pray for God's supernatural intervention.[26]

Many professionals and young people migrated from the country to find greener pastures abroad. I moved to the United States. For the young people who stayed behind, some who belonged to inter-denominational evangelical campus and school Christian fellowships emerged as leaders of the national prayer efforts. Prayer gave them hope. One scholar has argued that if the youth had despaired, the country could easily have faced a violent social revolution.[27]

The military government in power in 1981 had to negotiate a structural adjustment programme with the International Monetary Fund in the hope of reviving the economy, which did begin to recover by 2001. As Ghana's socio-economic and political situation stabilized, some of the more charismatic student leaders who had led the prayer fellowships of the 1970s grew their fellowships into churches. Some of these leaders had studied at the All Nations Bible Seminary in Benin City, Nigeria, a school that had been established by Benson Idahosa, a Pentecostal Charismatic Nigerian pastor.

Idahosa's Bible school offered scholarships to those who would otherwise not have been able to afford to attend. It thus became very influential in training and shaping the theology of many West African preachers. When they returned to Ghana after attending Idahosa's school, the former student leaders broke away from the more established

Pentecostal denominations, such as the Church of Pentecost and the Assemblies of God, and formed their own new churches. These new churches have continued to grow by leaps and bounds both in the country and in Ghanaian diaspora communities abroad.[28]

Idahosa had founded the Bible school and a large church with considerable financial support from American Pentecostal-Charismatic sources. These sources were part of a movement called the prosperity doctrine movement, or the faith movement.

THE AMERICAN PROSPERITY DOCTRINE

The origins of the modern prosperity doctrine can be traced to the teaching of E. W. Kenyon, a 20th-century American pastor. Kenyon, at various times affiliated with the Methodists, the Baptists, and various Pentecostal groups, drew the early principles of the prosperity doctrine from the New Thought cult teachings developed by Phineas P. Quimby (1802-66). Quimby used scientific language to make the non-Christian teachings of spiritism, occultism, and witchcraft acceptable in his cult.[29]

In the 1940s, Kenneth Hagin, a pastor of the American Assemblies of God, adopted and began to popularize aspects of Kenyon's teachings that are now associated with the prosperity doctrine.[30] In more recent years other American preachers who have promoted Hagin's prosperity teaching around the world include Oral Roberts, Kenneth Copeland and his wife Gloria, Fred Price, Jerry Savelle, John Avanzini, Benny Hinn, Creflo Dollar, Joel Osteen, and T. D. Jakes.

The television programmes and personal visits of these teachers introduced the prosperity doctrine to Africa. African preachers also studied abroad under these American prosperity preachers. Some of them founded some of Africa's currently fastest-growing new churches, preaching material blessing and deliverance.

APPEALING TO THE MIDDLE CLASS

As Ghana's socio-economic and political situation stabilized, a middle class of young upwardly mobile professionals began to emerge in the urban centres of the country. The theology of the new churches changed from its initial evangelical fervour to the more accommodative theology that emphasized material affluence and upward mobility. These churches offered to address the spiritual needs of Ghanaians that the older mission churches and the AICs seemed to have failed to meet during the years of economic and socio-political turbulence and decline.

> Perhaps unintentionally, these churches began to emphasize teachings about material affluence that kept the congregants and cash flowing in.

Social scientist Paul Gifford has studied these churches. He notes that many aspiring African middle-class professionals are drawn to the prosperity doctrine's promotion of "ambition, achievement and opportunity, directly geared to the upwardly mobile" and by prosperity teachers offering themselves as role models of "entrepreneurs who have developed" successful religious enterprises.[31] Sadly, they are not drawn to the church to find hope from the redemptive and transformative gospel message, because that is not what is offered there.

As these congregations grew and established institutional church structures, they needed to secure and reinforce sources of predictable income. Large church and administrative buildings, staff salaries, media programmes, church vehicles, musical instruments, and sound systems all had to be paid for and maintained on a regular basis. Perhaps unintentionally, these churches began to emphasize teachings about material affluence that kept the congregants and cash flowing in. They began to teach that people access the blessings and prosperity promised through faith, through sowing seeds – in other words, by giving their money to the church leaders. During my doctoral research, I remember the financial controller of one of these churches asking me pointedly, "How can we pay our bills and meet all our overhead expenses if we do not get church members to give?"

Churches have thus transitioned into commercial enterprises. Church leaders now function like business CEOs, measuring success by numerical growth. Church members have been turned into customers to be entertained by performances. Other churches are seen as business competitors. Evangelism resembles marketing. Church planting seems more like business franchising. Preaching now constitutes motivational speeches aimed at squeezing more money from church members.

Because many of these churches have elevated their church founders and leaders to the status of special "men of God" who possess special powers and anointing to solve all their congregants' spiritual and material difficulties, they also offer deliverance from witchcraft as part of their appeal to churchgoers. This strategy has seemed to work; more people give, more people come, and so they have kept doing it. By following this path, prosperity and deliverance have become the primary focus of their ministries. Loud, emotional services claim to be the work of the Holy Spirit, but the fruit of the Spirit is absent. Prayers frequently evoke the name of the Lord Jesus Christ, but his gospel is absent.

> Loud, emotional services claim to be the work of the Holy Spirit, but the fruit of the Spirit is absent. Prayers frequently evoke the name of the Lord Jesus Christ, but his gospel is absent.

Sadly, departing from the gospel, and replacing it with an emphasis on material blessing and deliverance from witchcraft has resulted in large numbers of unconverted second-generation churchgoers. But what our churches need is the truth of the gospel and genuine experiences of God's love and power.

Good News for the Poor

Ghana's story shows how times of economic and political instability can leave people desperate for hope. That hope can either be redirected towards God himself through the preaching of the true NT gospel, or it can stay focused on people's material needs and aspirations.

People faced with material needs can easily be led astray with promises of a better social status, health, freedom from anxiety about bills and household provisions, and the building of happy families. But false hope only disappoints.

The prosperity doctrine, ironically, keeps church members poor while their leaders get rich. It does not serve the poor; it only exploits them. Not only that, but it also fails to preach the message that would actually lead to transformed lives. Only the gospel convicts us of God's concern for both the spiritually and materially poor in our world. And only the gospel offers real hope to our broken continent.

People's needs can also be a great opportunity for the gospel. A study of church history shows that poor and vulnerable people have always been more eager to accept Christianity. They know they need God's help. God strongly identifies with the poor (Proverbs 14:31; 19:17; Matthew 25), even choosing to live among the poor. Jesus's birth was celebrated by shepherds, and he trained as an artisan before leaving for a full-time itinerant preaching ministry, where he didn't even have a place to lay his head (Matthew 8:20). At the beginning of his ministry, Jesus announced that his mission was "to proclaim good news to the poor" (Luke 4:18). He healed the sick and spoke out for the economically and politically deprived. Like many poor people today, he was a victim of gross injustice. He died without clothes at the hands of evil men and was buried in a borrowed tomb.[32] His immediate followers, the early

> The prosperity doctrine, ironically, keeps church members poor while their leaders get rich. It does not serve the poor; it only exploits them.

Christians, were persecuted, impoverished, and shamed for their countercultural faith (1 Corinthians 1:26-29).

The results of the gospel do not disappoint. I believe that if we saw people preach and apply the gospel of Jesus Christ in every area of our lives, we would see hearts and minds change. This could

Only the gospel offers real hope to our broken continent.

transform society. Imagine if corruption and exploitation were confessed and restitution made. The jealousy and fear of curses that hold us back would be defeated. In the long run, we could see Africa's vast material wealth begin to fulfil its potential, making a real difference in the lives of everyday people. We could see our continent rejuvenated socially, economically, and politically. But as Acts 3:19 reminds us, it is only when we repent and our sins are wiped out "that times of refreshing may come from the Lord."

However, if we are not careful, the church in Africa can turn our Christianity into a nice, safe middle-class religion that has left Christ and his gospel outside the door. The gospel challenged the rich and powerful in the early church to sacrifice and give up comfort. Then in the 4th century, the Roman Emperor Constantine embraced the faith and made Christianity the official religion of the Roman Empire. The church became an institution with official influence, power, and wealth. There was less emphasis on the gospel message, and more emphasis on religious dos and don'ts of socially acceptable behaviour. Church institutions and influential church leaders defended the status quo, even if it was unjust, greedy, and corrupt.

Church historian Andrew Walls explains that throughout the Christian centuries, wherever Christianity becomes associated with privilege and power, it becomes more concerned with preserving people's comfort. The gospel is abandoned, only for vulnerable people in another part of the world to discover its message and embrace it, bringing it to life anew in a different region. I believe this is why, today, the centre of Christianity has moved away from Europe towards places like Asia and Africa.[33] Now it is up to us: will the faith once for all delivered to the saints stay here and thrive, or will it move on? Will we lay aside our pursuit of power and privilege for the sake of the gospel or will we hold on to our comfort at the expense of our eternity? Will we focus on the blessings or the God who gives them?

> Wherever Christianity becomes associated with privilege and power, it becomes more concerned with preserving people's comfort.

Laodicea

The situation in the church in Africa today reminds me of the church in Laodicea in the first century. The church in Laodicea was one of seven churches that the Lord addressed with both words of commendation and words of correction at the beginning of the book of Revelation.

The Lord told them: "Here I am! I stand at the door and knock. If anyone hears my voice and opens the door, I will come in and eat with that person, and they with me" (Revelation 3:20). As the Laodicean Christians carried on with their well-meaning church services and as they busily engaged in all their religious practices, they did not realize that they had left Christ outside the church. Christ calls from outside, asking them to hear and let him in. This is quite a sobering picture.

In the first century, Laodicea was a wealthy banking centre. Their main products were a special eye medicine and glossy black wool from its sheep used for manufacturing expensive clothing and carpets. The city also had a famous medical school that attracted students from across the Roman Empire. Laodicea was so wealthy that, in AD 60, when the city was almost destroyed by a very severe earthquake, the city leaders refused relief from the Roman Senate because Laodicea's rich banking firms were confident that they could finance the reconstruction of the city themselves.

This pride in their wealth made the Laodicean church describe itself: "I am rich; I have acquired wealth and do not need a thing" (Revelation 3:17). But in the second half of the same verse, the Lord saw them as "wretched, pitiful, poor, blind and naked." What a contrast! The church boasted about its material wealth, but the Lord saw only its spiritual poverty!

Will we focus on the blessings or the God who gives them?

To the north of Laodicea, streams of soda-laden warm water ran into the river in the south, near Laodicea. Medical tourists came regularly to Laodicea from across the Roman world to drink the water in hopes of being healed of their various ailments. But during certain seasons of the year, as the hot water flowed down the slopes, it quickly became lukewarm, so that it lost its supposed healing power. It became good for nothing! When the Lord called the Laodiceans "lukewarm", he was telling them that they had become good for nothing spiritually.

The Lord didn't end there. The "poor" Laodiceans needed to stop boasting about their wealth of gold and money and buy spiritual gold, which represented faith and obedience. The "blind" Laodiceans needed to stop boasting about their special eye medicine and receive spiritual sight from the Lord so that they might see their spiritual poverty. The "naked" Laodiceans needed to stop boasting about their expensive wool clothing and obtain white clothes from the Lord that represent righteousness and purity. The Lord was telling the Laodiceans in terms they could understand to be honest about their true spiritual condition.

The Lord's call to the Laodicean church to humbly repent evidently fell on deaf ears. Today if you go to the Turkish city Denizli, where the Laodicean church was located in the first century, you will find no trace of the church. It still has a significant textile production

Could our churches be courting the fate of the church in Western countries?

industry. The hot springs still attract tourists to spa hotels. But there is no church there. The Lord warned that he would spit them out of his mouth because they were neither hot nor cold (Revelation 3:16).

These were Christians whom the Lord loved dearly, which was why he was rebuking and disciplining them (Revelation 3:19). If the Laodicean Christians humbled themselves before the Lord and repented, the Lord promised that he would give them the right to sit with him on his throne (Revelation 3:21-22).

As the emphasis in churches in Africa today moves away from the original NT gospel of Christ to material wealth, could our churches be courting the fate of the church in Laodicea, and more recently, the fate of the church in Western countries? Have we pushed Christ and his gospel so far out of our churches that he is knocking at the door asking to be let back in?

Questions for Reflection and Discussion

1. What similarities and differences do you notice when you compare your country's history with Ghana's recent church history?

2. How do times of economic and political instability provide opportunities for the gospel? How do such situations provide opportunities for false teaching?

3. How does economic growth or middle-class affluence provide opportunities for the gospel? How do such situations provide opportunities for false teaching?

Strategy

CHAPTER 4

IMMORALITY AND DENYING THE LORD

For certain individuals whose condemnation was written
about long ago have secretly slipped in among you.
They are ungodly people, who pervert the grace of
our God into a licence for immorality and deny
Jesus Christ our only Sovereign and Lord (Jude 4).

Several years ago, I was on the leadership team of a Bible study fellowship in a large Pentecostal church in Nairobi. Some of my fellow leaders decided to invite a prominent West African prosperity and motivation teacher to speak to the church. We were all asked to contribute to pay for the leader's visit. I had misgivings, but another leader I respected persuaded me. He was personally acquainted with the teacher's ministry and was sure the man's visit would be a blessing to the church.

On the first night of teaching, I took a taxi to the event in the church. The taxi driver was a friend of mine and I tried to persuade him to stay for the event. He had another client to pick up, he said, but he promised he would pick me up after the event.

The West African teacher walked into the pulpit without a Bible and spoke for two hours without once referring to Christ and the gospel. He spoke of his rise from rags to riches. "If you want to achieve your potential," he said to the packed church hall, "choose your friends carefully. Make friends with people of power and influence who can propel you to greatness. Do not make friends with taxi drivers and barbers and people like that. What can you get from such people?"

I was horrified. I quietly thanked God that my taxi driver friend had not been able to come. I couldn't believe I had financially supported this man's visit to the country. His two other talks that weekend were no better. They focused on himself, his success, and the need for Christians to emulate the material success of non-Christians. It made me especially sad that the other leaders of the fellowship didn't seem to regret inviting this man to speak to the church.

False Teachers

PERMISSION TO BE IMMORAL

Still in verse 4, Jude writes that the false teachers who had infiltrated the church showed no reverence for God. They changed the grace of God into a licence for immorality. In other words, they taught that since God's grace covered sin, people were free to be immoral. Their thinking and lifestyles displayed the immorality that Christ spoke against (Mark 7:21-22).

Jude's description suggests that these false teachers were influenced by an early form of a heresy that would eventually become known as Gnosticism. But strong Gnostic ideas were already prevalent during the first century when Jude wrote. Gnosticism was a religious philosophy that taught that God was spirit and good, and that matter and the world were hopelessly evil. Therefore, God could not have created the physical world, because good cannot create evil. It taught that a lesser divinity, called the Demiurge, made the mistake of forming the world, in which souls, as divine sparks, are imprisoned and asleep.

Gnosticism taught that the physical world was bad and without remedy. One's true divine self was imprisoned in the evil physical human body. Special, secret knowledge was the key to freeing oneself.

Gnosticism, therefore, led to two different lifestyles. Some Gnostics "denied the flesh", shunning worldly things. They tried to overcome physical desires, purify their spirits, and hasten their release from the prison of the body.

Other Gnostics concluded that since they were spiritual beings imprisoned in physical bodies, it made no difference what they did with their bodies if they kept themselves spiritually pure. This second group therefore often behaved immorally and took no responsibility for their behaviour.[34] This is probably the group Jude was addressing because, in verse 8, Jude accuses the false teachers of polluting their bodies on the strength of their dreams.

We see this Gnostic tendency among false teachers today whose lifestyles display greed and immorality. A few years ago, my wife and I were eating dinner at a Chinese restaurant when we saw a well-known Kenyan prosperity preacher at a nearby table. Accompanying him was a very attractive woman in high heels, dressed in tight and revealing clothes that accentuated her figure. We knew his wife, but this was another woman. She looked to be at least a decade younger than the preacher. Two other men also sat at the table, each with a much younger woman. The preacher and his wife had been mentored by a dear friend of ours. It was heartbreaking to see him shamelessly and publicly entertaining a woman who was not his wife.

Some time later, on a trip to Ghana, I saw this preacher on a huge poster advertising a conference organized by one of the local churches that teaches the prosperity doctrine. He had been invited to be one of the speakers along with other foreign and local prosperity teachers. His spiritual talk was utterly disconnected from living a holy life in his physical body, resembling the false teachers in Jude's time.

DENYING CHRIST AND HIS WORD

Jude also describes the false teachers as denying Jesus Christ. Gnosticism taught that if Christ was the true spiritual God, he could not have had a physical body, which they associated with evil. The Gnostics believed Christ appeared to be human, but his body was not a real human body. This teaching threatened to turn Jesus into a myth. It also threatened the core of the gospel message, because if Christ was not a human being, he could not have died on behalf of all humans.

The leaders of the early church strongly rejected this, insisting that Jesus's human nature was real. Paul said Jesus was "born of a woman" (Galatians 4:4). The early church emphasized the virgin birth of Christ to stress both his divinity and his very real humanity. John said that in Jesus, "the Word became flesh" and was "heard, . . . seen . . . looked at . . . [and] touched" (John 1:14; 1 John 1:1-2).

Gnostic teachers also denied Christ by redefining biblical terms to fit their narrative of how people find salvation. The term *redeemer* is an example. In the Bible, Christ redeems or saves humans from sin and sin's penalty of death, through his sacrificial death and resurrection. In the Gnostic view, however, Christ redeems or saves human beings from bondage to the material world through imparting special knowledge.

Albert Bell explains that to support this teaching, the Gnostics imported their own meaning into various NT passages, regardless of what these texts meant in their original contexts. Jesus said that he was the way and the truth, and that knowing the truth would make people free (John 8:32; 14:6). He thanked God "for hiding these things from those who think themselves wise and clever, and for revealing them to the childlike" (Matthew 11:25). The Gnostics took these texts as evidence that Jesus had come to offer them the knowledge that would enable their imprisoned souls to break free of their physicality. In Luke 23:49, the Greek word for Jesus's friends who watched the crucifixion is *gnostoi*. While the word only means "those who knew him", the Gnostics claimed it meant Jesus was the Gnostic redeemer who gave special knowledge.[35]

Gnostic teachers went further than misinterpreting Scripture out of context. One prominent Gnostic teacher called Marcion went so far as to reject entire parts of the Bible because they did not say what he wanted to hear. Marcion taught that God was a God of love, not of law, and therefore, the Old Testament God was not the true God, but the Demiurge. So, Marcion rejected the entire Old Testament. He accepted as Scripture only 10 of Paul's letters and an edited version of Luke's Gospel (stripping out some Jewish elements), because of Luke's association with Paul. Marcion influenced cities all over the Roman Empire. In response, the church decided they needed to define which books were officially the canon of the church. The church excommunicated Marcion in Rome in AD 144 for his Gnostic teaching.[36]

While this happened after Jude's time, Jude's urgency shows he realized just how dangerous the false teachers could become if the church did not stop them immediately. The false teachers ignored what Scripture taught about immorality. They didn't submit to God's Word. They took out of context the grace of God and the truth that

Jesus was God. They ignored the rest of the apostles' teaching and the prophecies about Jesus that taught clearly that Jesus was human. The gospel was clearly at stake.

Twisting Scripture

I see a similarity between the false teachers we just described and how people misuse and refuse to obey the Scriptures today. Just because someone quotes Scripture does not necessarily mean he or she is in line with God's Word or God's will. Satan quoted Psalm 91 out of context (Luke 4:9-12). He tried to tempt Christ Jesus to prove he was the Son of God by throwing himself off the Temple so that the angels would come and rescue him. But Jesus knew that this was not God's will, and he replied by quoting another Scripture correctly: "Do not put the Lord your God to the test." Scripture must be correctly interpreted, as God intended it in the original context, to be rightly considered the Word of God.[37] Then, we must obey it.

First, let's understand what it means to interpret the Bible accurately. Randy Hedlun says, "reading the Bible is much like eavesdropping on a group of foreigners"[38] – they speak an unfamiliar language and come from a culture we do not understand. The Bible was written long ago by authors who came from cultures with languages and worldviews that were very different from our own. The original readers of the books in the Bible came from the same cultures as the authors of these books, so they more easily understood what the authors meant.

> Just because someone quotes Scripture does not necessarily mean they are in line with God's Word or God's will.

Today, it takes more effort for us to understand what they meant to communicate. But God, in his sovereign wisdom, chose which authors, languages, and cultures he wanted to use to communicate his message. So, it is our God-given responsibility to become familiar with their historical, literary, social, and religious contexts if we want to understand his Word and how to apply it in today's world.[39]

This is why the accurate interpretation of the Word of God requires that we find out the original meaning of the text as it was intended by the original author, and as it was understood by his original readers. This is done through a careful study of the text's historical, cultural, and literary contexts.

> It is our God-given responsibility to become familiar with the Bible's historical, literary, social, and religious contexts if we want to understand his Word.

Let's look at some examples of frequently misused Scriptures to understand these principles better.

3 JOHN 2

Some people teach that 3 John 2 claims that God wishes material and financial prosperity and health for all Christians. In the KJV, it says, "Beloved, I wish above all things that thou mayest prosper and be in health, even as thy soul prospereth." However, in the apostle John's culture, at the time, his phrase was simply a standard form of greeting in letters, much like "I trust this email finds you well." That is why more recent translations like the NIV say, "I pray that you may enjoy good health and that all may go well with you, just as you are progressing spiritually." Usually, if someone's interpretation of a Scripture only works with one Bible translation, that means they have taken the Scripture out of context.

MARK 10:29-30

To accurately interpret the Word of God, you need to look at the whole chapter containing that verse and how it connects to other parts of the Bible. If you only look at one verse, you could get the wrong impression about what the verse is saying.

For instance, some people use Jesus's statement about a hundredfold return in Mark 10:29-30 to say that Christians who give money to their ministries will reap a hundredfold financial return. This is the verse:

> 'Truly I tell you,' Jesus replied, 'no one who has left home or brothers or sisters or mother or father or children or fields for me and the gospel will fail to receive a hundred times as much in this present age: homes, brothers, sisters, mothers, children and fields – along with persecutions – and in the age to come eternal life.'

To accurately interpret the Word of God, you need to look at the whole chapter containing that verse and how it connects to other parts of the Bible.

If you look at the context, just before this, a rich man came to ask what he must do to inherit eternal life, now that he had obeyed all the commandments. Jesus told him, "Go, sell everything you have and give to the poor, and you will have treasure in heaven. Then come, follow me" (Mark 10:21). The man was not supposed to sell his possessions to give them to Jesus or another Christian leader. He was supposed to give them to the poor.

Peter responded, "We have left everything to follow you!" He was probably remembering how he had left his fishing business, his wife, and his mother-in-law to follow Jesus around the countryside as he taught. Jesus responded with the verse quoted above. He reassured Peter that the cost of being a disciple was worth it, but he also warned him that he should expect persecution. We know that Peter was jailed at least three times (Acts 4:3; 5:17-32; 12:4) and flogged (5:40). Church tradition teaches that Peter was crucified by the Romans.

Correctly interpreted, Jesus's statement was about the cost of discipleship, not its financial advantages. If it inspires people to give, their giving should be to the poor. People who use it to encourage people to give to themselves and their ministries, promising that their investment will be returned 100 times, are clearly misusing this Scripture. They are deceiving people into giving them money and encouraging them to be greedy.

PSALM 90:10 – A GUARANTEED LIFESPAN?

Psalm 90:10 says, "Our days may come to seventy years, or eighty, if our strength endures; yet the best of them are but trouble and sorrow, for they quickly pass, and we fly away." This verse is often misinterpreted to mean that God has decreed the normal human life expectancy to be 80 years. A careful study of this text's historical, cultural, and literary contexts, however, yields a very different meaning.

The title of this Psalm reveals that it was a prayer of Moses. After the Israelites' deliverance from Egypt, on their way to the Promised Land, they discovered that the Promised Land was inhabited by people who were physically much bigger and stronger than they were. They rebelled against Moses, their God-appointed leader (Numbers 13–14). The Israelites were expressing their lack of faith in God's ability to fulfil his promise to settle them in the Promised Land, even though he had miraculously delivered them from Egypt.

As a result of their unbelief, God responded that it would take the Israelites 40 years to enter the land of promise, and none of the adults aged 20 and above would live long enough to arrive in Canaan (Numbers 14:20-35). God carried out his judgement; over the next 40 years of their journey through the wilderness, all the adult Israelites died as they approached the age of 70 or 80. Only Joshua and Caleb lived beyond the age of 80 years to possess the land (Joshua 14:6-13) because they did not join in the rebellion but had faith in the Lord's ability to settle the Israelites in the land as he had promised.

During the wilderness journey, Moses watched the adults die in the wilderness for their unbelief. Deeply grieved, Moses prayed to God the words we have in Psalm 90. This explains why Moses writes:

> All our days pass away under your wrath;
>> we finish our years with a moan . . .
> If only we knew the power of your anger!
>> Your wrath is as great as the fear that is your due.
> Teach us to number our days,
>> that we may gain a heart of wisdom (Psalm 90:9, 11-12).

Identify timeless implications and principles that can be applied in the context of contemporary Christians.

Accurately interpreting Scripture also means paying attention to who is talking, and to whom. God wasn't speaking out a promise or a blessing of a specific lifespan for everyone in Psalm 90:10. Instead, Moses was describing their difficult situation and pleading with God on behalf of the people he was leading: "Relent, Lord, how long will it be? Have compassion on your servants" (Psalm 90:13).

After carefully studying the historical, cultural, and literary context of a text, you have a better understanding of the author's original intention. Based on this, you can identify timeless implications and principles that can be applied in the historical, social, and spiritual context of contemporary Christians.

We can apply Psalm 90:10 to Christians today by saying that we need to learn from the Israelites' unbelief to exercise faith in God, even when what God has promised seems impossible from a human point of view. Can you see how different this is from the incorrect but commonly held interpretation that God has decreed a lifespan of 80 years for human beings?

DEUTERONOMY 28:1-14 – THE BLESSING OF PROSPERITY?

To accurately interpret God's Word, we also need to discover how we are different from, or similar to, the original audience addressed in a Bible text. For instance, in Deuteronomy 28:1-14 God promises to bless Israel with material prosperity if they obey the old covenant:

> You will be blessed in the city and blessed in the country . . .
> You will be blessed when you come in and blessed when you go
> out. The Lord will grant that the enemies who rise up against
> you will be defeated before you. They will come at you from one
> direction but flee from you in seven . . . The Lord will make
> you the head, not the tail . . . you will always be at the top, never
> at the bottom. (Deuteronomy 28:3, 6-7, 13)

Many Christians today claim these promises. But how similar are we to the original audience? This OT text was written to Jews who experienced their relationship with God in the context of the Old Covenant. The law of the Old Covenant offered blessing if the Israelites obeyed God, as these verses in this passage demonstrate:

> . . . The Lord will establish you as his holy people, as he
> promised you on oath, *if you keep the commands of the Lord
> your God and walk in obedience to him.* Then all the peoples on
> earth will see that you are called by the name of the Lord, and
> they will fear you. The Lord will grant you abundant prosperity
> – in the fruit of your womb, the young of your livestock and the
> crops of your ground – in the land he swore to your ancestors
> to give you.

. . . The Lord will make you the head, not the tail. *If you pay attention to the commands of the Lord your God that I give you this day and carefully follow them*, you will always be at the top, never at the bottom (Deuteronomy 28:9-11, 13, emphasis added).

Unfortunately, the original Israelites to whom these words were addressed were unable to obey the law. With few exceptions, they received the curses rather than the blessings.

However, most Christians today are Gentile believers, so we are no longer under the Old Covenant. Our relationship with God is in the context of the New Covenant established by the work of Christ on the cross for us. As Christians, we come to God not through our good works, but through faith in Jesus, who has freed us from the law and its curses (Galatians 2:15–3:14).

Some may ask, but do the blessings still apply to us? The blessings were part of God's mission strategy in the OT. He would materially bless Israel, his covenant people, if they obeyed him. Then the pagan Gentile nations around them could come and see and know that the God of Israel was the one true God. Verse 10 of the passage above demonstrates this: "Then all the peoples on earth will see that you are called by the name of the Lord, and they will fear you." Another example is when Solomon dedicates the Temple. He prays that foreigners would hear about God's glory, come and pray towards the Temple, and the nations would know the Lord as a result (1 Kings 8:41-43, 59-60). A well-known and prominent African prosperity preacher assumed this mission strategy applied today when he famously claimed that God's mission today is to "make my people rich."[40]

In the NT, Jesus changes the mission strategy from "come-see" to "go-tell". After his resurrection, and just before his ascension, he gives his disciples the Great Commission, commanding them to "go and make disciples of all nations" in Matthew 28:18-20.[41] While it is true that God still blesses people today, we can't claim promises such as Deuteronomy 28 are an eternal guarantee that Christians will have material prosperity.

> Have our churches become so busy with what we perceive to be the work of the Lord that we have neglected the Lord of the work?

During my doctoral research, I visited many impressive church buildings and offices. Many churches today define success by the construction of these worship palaces. But we are no longer living in the times of Solomon, where God dwells in a Temple and brings the nations to one central location to worship him. We are in the times of the apostles, where God sends us out to the nations without even an extra shirt so that we depend on the generosity of others (Matthew 10:9-10). Misinterpreting these Scriptures has caused our churches to become so busy with what we perceive to be the work of the Lord that we have neglected the Lord of the work. We need to return to his gospel of redemption and transformation.

Obeying God and His Word

God's Word clearly condemned the immoral behaviour of the false teachers in Jude. They did not interpret it accurately and they did not want to obey it. They made up all sorts of rationales to justify their refusal to submit to God's Word. This demonstrated that they did not submit to Christ as Lord.

Preachers especially must place themselves and their message under the authority of the Word of God, or they lose credibility with their hearers. After the 2007 disputed Kenyan general elections, a wave of post-election violence swept across the country. Different political parties pitted ethnic communities against one another in politically instigated bloodletting that left more than 1,000 people dead across the country. Entire communities were also pressed into

> Preachers especially must place themselves and their message under the authority of the Word of God, or they lose credibility with their hearers.

camps for internally displaced people across the country.

Unfortunately, the ethnic fault lines of this political conflict appeared in the church. One pastor I know tried to address the sharp ethnic divisions that had suddenly emerged among the members of his congregation by preaching a series of sermons about reconciliation.

At that same time, a rift arose between this pastor and the treasurer of the church. The two men exchanged harsh words. The treasurer was so emotionally wounded by this conflict that he left the church, although he was still willing to reconcile with the pastor. But all efforts to get the pastor to reconcile with the treasurer failed.

Although the pastor was preaching a series of sermons on ethnic reconciliation, this pastor refused to submit to the very Word of God that he was preaching and reconcile with his treasurer. Many church members noticed that what this pastor was preaching and what he was practising did not match. So, they responded to his preaching with disillusionment, cynicism, and indifference.

Denying that Jesus is Lord

During the cold winter months, a man was in the habit of drinking wine with his meals, and he tended to drink to excess. One summer, the late Christian leader, Watchman Nee, led the man and his wife to the Lord. A new light and joy came into their lives.

One evening when the winter returned, the wine came back to the table. The husband bowed to pray for the meal, but no words would come out of his mouth.

After a few more tries, the man asked his wife, "What's wrong? Why can't we pray today? Fetch the Bible and see what it has to say about wine-drinking."

She turned the Bible's pages, but didn't find any answers. Watchman Nee was many miles away and it might be months before they could consult him.

"Just drink your wine," said his wife. "We'll ask Brother Nee at the first opportunity." But still the man found he just couldn't give thanks to the Lord for that wine.

"Take it away!" he finally said and at last they asked a blessing on their meal.

Eventually the man shared the story with Watchman Nee, saying, "Resident Boss wouldn't let me have that drink!"

"Very good, brother," replied the Christian leader. "You always listen to Resident Boss!"[42] The "Resident Boss," of course, was the Lord Jesus Christ, whose life the Holy Spirit had imparted to the couple at their conversion. Christ Jesus is not only our Saviour, but also our Lord and Master (Philippians 2:10-11).

Jude writes in verse 4 that the "individuals" who had come into the church were denying Jesus Christ as our only Sovereign and Lord. The false teachers wanted Christ to be their servant, not their Lord and master. They wanted Christ to meet their needs without telling them what to do.[43] They demonstrated unacceptable insubordination to God. Jesus said, "Whoever does not honour the Son does not honour the Father, who sent him" (John 5:23). Christ "must be Lord of all, or He is not Lord at all."[44]

The entire NT is categorical that Jesus Christ is Lord (Romans 10:9; 1 Corinthians 12:3; Philippians 2:11; 1 Peter 3:15). By raising Christ from the dead, God the Father once and for all declared, "Jesus is Lord" (Romans 1:3-4). Paul writes, "Christ died and returned to life so that he might be the Lord of both the dead and the living" (Romans 14:9). Christians talk about "making" Christ "Lord," but Peter makes it clear that "God has made this Jesus, whom you crucified, both Lord and Christ" (Acts 2:36, NKJV). God has exalted

> The false teachers wanted Christ to be their servant, not their Lord and master. They wanted Christ to meet their needs without telling them what to do.

him so that every tongue must confess that Jesus is Lord (Philippians 2:9-11). God has made him Lord, not us, and therefore we must come to terms with Christ as our Lord.[45]

One afternoon shortly after I moved to Nairobi, I was driving on the road to the airport. A police officer stopped me for speeding. I explained that I did not know what the speed limit was for that road and that there were no signs along the road informing motorists of the speed limit. He could tell that I was new to the city because I didn't have a Kenyan driver's licence, and he allowed me to go.

Still, the fact that the country I had just come from had higher speed limits did not exempt me from submitting to the speed limit in Kenya, whether I knew what that speed limit was or not. In this same way, the lordship of Christ is an established fact, whether we believe it or not, or whether we submit to him or not. Our issue is not making Christ Lord, but submitting to him as Lord.

In Jude's epistle, the false teachers' denial of the Lord had to do with their Gnostic teachings that Christ was not human. If he was not human, he could not have died on behalf of all humans. So then salvation would no longer be through trusting and believing in Christ, but through one's own efforts to purify oneself. We have already discussed how religious efforts to become right with God fundamentally misunderstand the gospel.

Christ can make a claim on our lives as Lord because he came from heaven to earth to make it possible for us to go from earth to heaven. He came to live the life we should have lived, but could not, on account of our sinfulness. He died the death we should have died, on account of our sinfulness, so that we might be forgiven by the

Father, and never be forsaken by the Father. He came in weakness to serve and to save us. This is how he changed the world and our lives. This is why he is our Sovereign and Lord, and this is why Jude calls the false teachers to account for denying Christ as our only Sovereign and Lord.

One example I see of not respecting Christ as Lord is when we recite the name of Jesus as a kind of talisman that we should expect to bring us good fortune. Jesus's name becomes a tool to accomplish the results we want – deliverance, healing, or success. By misusing his name, we ask him to submit to us and our will. But Christ is our Lord and Master, the Lord of the Word in the Word of the Lord. It is we who must submit to him and his Word.

When We Don't Submit

> Our issue is not making Christ Lord, but submitting to him as Lord.

Like the men whom Jude denounces so strongly in his epistle for their immorality, we too often today read sordid stories in the media about the involvement of prosperity teachers in various financial and sexual scandals.

In recent years, I heard again of the West African preacher who spoke to the Pentecostal church in Nairobi. He had gained a position of prominence on the board of directors of a bank in his home country. The bank failed. The government's regulatory banking body investigated. They discovered that the bank had failed partly because this church leader and other members of the bank's board had illegally awarded themselves large loans that they could not repay. The government has brought criminal charges against them.

Many observers attributed the church leader's unfortunate role in this scandal to his many years of teaching about material prosperity. He had elevated money to the status of a god and made it an idol in his life. These critical, and perhaps unkind, observers claimed that the man became a victim of his own teaching. At the very least,

I knew from the moment he spoke for two hours without a Bible in that church in Nairobi that he did not care about submitting to God's Word or making Christ Lord. It was not a surprise to me that financial immorality was the result of this attitude.

Questions for Reflection and Discussion

1. Have you heard any of the verses described in this chapter misused? What have you learned from these explanations?

2. What other examples of commonly used verses can you think of? Take time to look up some of these verses. Read them, then read the whole chapter where they are found. Ask who is speaking to whom. You may need to look at the surrounding chapters or the beginning of the book to figure that out. What do you think the original readers were supposed to understand by these verses?

3. Like the pastor preaching on reconciliation, when have you found yourself saying one thing, but living differently? Ask God to help you to obey his Word and submit to his Lordship.

Trust in the Lord

CHAPTER 5
FAITH VERSUS UNBELIEF

Though you already know all this, I want to remind you
that the Lord at one time delivered his people out of Egypt,
but later destroyed those who did not believe (Jude 5).

It was a bright sun-filled Sunday morning. The large church hall was packed with congregants wearing their Sunday best.

"Faith is all you need!" The church founder had been preaching for almost half an hour by now. "You need to have faith in yourself. You need to have faith in your dreams, faith in your hard work, faith in your pastors, faith in your mentors, faith in those who have gone ahead of you. Faith will translate your dreams into reality. Without faith it will not happen, trust me! This is how we got to where we are today. Faith, my friends, faith!" He spoke emphatically and with great conviction.

This was another new and fast-growing church in the country. It was impressively large and modern, with an adjoining building for the youth and children's ministries that also housed classrooms for a kindergarten. Above the hall were suites of offices.

I had attended this service that Sunday morning as part of my continuing doctoral research. As the founding pastor went on and on, I was glad I had attended the service with two close relatives because, without their presence with me, I would easily have left the service in the middle of the long sermon. I was depressed by both the message and how the church members seated around me paid such rapt, respectful attention to it.

> In Mark 11:22, Jesus said, "Have faith in God." He did not say that we should have faith in our faith.

In verse 5, Jude warns his readers not to be like the Israelites, who did not believe. Many churches today, like the one I visited, are full of frequent calls to have faith. But how does this call to have faith compare with what Jude meant when he called his readers to have faith?

Faith in Faith

At the heart of the prosperity doctrine preached in many churches across Africa today is the teaching that people can have whatever they desire through a positive confession of faith. In the early years of the prosperity doctrine's development, Kenneth Hagin conceived a formula of positive confession that consists of "saying it, doing it, receiving it, and telling it."[46] Hagin claimed that anyone who applied these four principles of faith would receive whatever they wanted, whether they were Christians or not. This doctrine thus advocates faith in one's faith. This is a direct contradiction of the teaching of the Bible. In Mark 11:22, Jesus said, "Have faith in God." He did not say that we should have faith in our faith.

African churchgoers are easy prey for prosperity teaching because they often bring lingering aspects of an ATR worldview into the church with them. In this worldview they struggle daily with spirit beings. They put a great deal of faith in rituals and the witchdoctor's costly sacrifices to cajole, appease, placate, and manipulate the spirits. When believers in ATR become Christians, they are not really moving from no faith to faith. They are moving from wrong faith to right faith, from false gods to the one true God, embracing the gospel truth that their new Lord is far greater than the evil spirit beings that previously held sway over their lives.[47]

In the Bible, faith is an attitude of trust that we adopt towards something or someone which enables that thing to function in accordance with its qualities or the person to function in accordance with their character. Faith does not exist in itself; it is always an attitude towards an object or person. Faith in God is therefore an attitude of trust in God that enables him "to be what he is and to do what only he can do in our experience."[48] Our faith in God, therefore, is based on what he has revealed himself to be to us both in Scripture and in our own experience. Faith in God is never blind trust. It is always based on the revealed, known character of God in whom we place our trust.

This means that, contrary to much erroneous teaching in our churches today, the important factor in our faith is not its size or magnitude, but rather its object, which must always be God himself. Clearly, this is what Christ meant when he said in Matthew 17:20, "Truly I tell you, if you have faith as small as a mustard seed, you can say to this mountain, 'Move from here to there,' and it will move. Nothing will be impossible for you." Christ is saying that the size of your faith doesn't matter. It is the almighty God in whom our

> The important factor in our faith is not its size or magnitude, but rather its object, which must always be God himself.

mustard seed faith is placed, who removes from our lives our mountains of needs and difficulties.

Shipwrecking Faith

In verses 12 and 13, Jude describes the false teachers who had come into the church by writing, "These people are blemishes at your love feasts, eating with you without the slightest qualm – shepherds who feed only themselves."

Love feasts in Jude refers to the early church tradition of partaking in the Holy Communion when they met.[49] Because the Greek word translated here as *blemishes* can also be translated as *hidden rocks,* Jude is implying that these men whose teaching departed from the gospel were like dangerous hidden reefs that could shipwreck the faith of his readers.[50]

A couple of years ago, a fellow member of my Bible study fellowship constantly asked the group to pray for his sister. This sister had come under the spell of one of Kenya's charismatic prosperity preachers. She constantly "sowed seeds", giving all her earnings away to the preacher's church. Her family was left destitute. They were dependent on handouts from her siblings to meet her financial needs and obligations.

The prosperity preacher owns a fleet of flashy four-wheel-drive vehicles. He is driven around Nairobi with a motorcade of minders and bodyguards and is married to two wives. I once came across his motorcade when one of the cars in that motorcade had been involved in an accident with a motorcycle. The preacher's bodyguards were threatening to lynch the frightened motorcycle rider.

Prosperity preachers blame churchgoers for their lack of faith as a way of excusing their inability to make real their false promises to churchgoers.

Like the sister of my Bible study colleague, many churchgoers in Africa today desperately pour all their resources and time into church, causing problems for their work, their marriages, their education, and their families. Offered promises of wealth and health by their pastors, when miraculous provision does not materialize, churchgoers are accused of lacking faith.

The simple truth is that prosperity preachers blame churchgoers for their lack of faith as a way of excusing their inability to make real their false promises to churchgoers. As the Cameroonian Bible scholar, Dieudonné Tamfu, put it, "These preachers twist Scriptures in order to twist the arms of their followers for money. They distort to extort . . . They seduce before they swindle."[51]

> Churchgoers are made to feel cursed when their difficult financial circumstances prevent them from sowing the so-called seeds of faith through tithes and offerings.

These unfortunate practices have sadly turned many Africans away from the church altogether, and some have even turned to Islam. In one stark, graphic, and alarming illustration of this sad reality, on March 16th, 2020, an article in a Ugandan newspaper reported a story about the arrest of a man who burned down three churches in Kasokoso Kira Municipality in Wakiso District, Uganda, because the churches regularly preached prosperity and yet this had failed to get him out of poverty in spite of the many years he had faithfully paid money to those churches.[52]

As in Jude's day, false teaching today only offers false hope and disappointment to churchgoers in Africa. Churchgoers are made to feel cursed when their difficult financial circumstances prevent them from sowing the so-called seeds of faith through tithes and offerings. Churchgoers feel a sense of abandonment and diminished self-worth when they are accused of lacking faith because their so-called miracles of provision do not materialize as promised by prosperity preachers. Sadly, these churchgoers are not taught that the gospel alone offers them the real and tangible hope they seek.

The absence of the gospel in these churches means that churchgoers are denied the assuring implication of the gospel that because, for our sake, God the Father did not spare Christ, but gave him up for us all, he will also graciously give us all things that he knows we need (Romans 8:32). They are not taught the firm gospel promise that, in Christ, our heavenly Father knows what we need before we ask him, and that he will readily provide to us everything that he knows is good for us that we ask of him in believing prayer (Matthew 6:8, 33). The false teachers' false promises lead people's faith to shipwreck.

They are also shipwrecking the faith by souring the attitudes of non-Christians towards the church. Print media, and more recently, social media, frequently criticize these churches as nothing other than a commercial enterprise to enrich its founders.[53] In 2016, the Kenyan government, for example, introduced "a raft of tough new measures" to change the way religious institutions such as churches are run in the country.[54] This was the government's response to "widespread public outrage" over reports of fake miracles and promises made by some Kenyan church leaders to defraud the public.[55] Our Christian witness in Africa is increasingly at stake.

Israel's Unbelief

So, what does faith look like according to Jude? He shows us by describing its opposite: unbelief. In verse 5, he refers to the story of God's divine act of salvation for his OT people from their bondage in Egypt. The Israelites had been slaves, but God had inflicted plagues on Egypt until Pharaoh let them go. When Pharaoh pursued them with his army, God performed an amazing miracle, enabling Israel to cross the Red Sea but drowning the Egyptian army when they tried to follow. After God had saved the Israelites by his grace, the appropriate response would have been faith in God and thanksgiving to him.

Instead, their response became the role model for unbelief. In Psalm 95, 1 Corinthians 10:1-12, and Hebrews 3–4, the biblical authors held it up as the ultimate warning. When Moses went up the mountain to receive the Law, the people made a golden calf in his absence and worshipped it as an idol. Every time they ran out of water or got tired of their food, they threatened to go back to Egypt. God provided for them over and over, but they complained instead of trusting him (Exodus 15:24; 17:3; Numbers 14:29). Jude compares the false teachers to the Israelites in verse 16 by calling them "grumblers and fault-finders."

When God was about to bring Israel into the Promised Land, Moses sent out 12 spies ahead to survey the land God was giving to them. But Israel was afraid of the people they would need to fight. The people wished, once again, that they had never left Egypt. At this point, God told them they would stay 40 years in the wilderness for their unbelief. Jude reminds his readers of this to drive home the danger of unbelief.

To emphasize his point, in verses 6 and 7, Jude refers to God's OT judgements, such as God's spectacular destruction of Sodom and Gomorrah and the surrounding towns (Genesis 19:1-25). In verse 11, he recalls an incident where Korah and his confederates led a rebellion against Moses and Aaron's divinely appointed authority, and God caused the earth to give way beneath their feet, swallowing them alive (Numbers 16).

> God wants us to trust that he is merciful and that he cares very deeply for us.

Jude's reference to God's severe judgement of the unbelieving Israelites was his reminder to his readers, and to us today, that the primary thing God wants from us is trust. God wants us to trust that he is merciful and that he cares very deeply for us. To see this, all we need to do is to remind ourselves of the message at the heart of the gospel that God became incarnate in the person of Jesus Christ to take our place of punishment and condemnation on the cross. Why would we hesitate to trust a God who has done this for us?

Faith When We Fear Enemies

Like the Israelites, we find it very hard to trust God, especially when we have unmet needs or when we suffer, like the Israelites complaining about their food, or when we face fearful enemies as the Israelites did when the spies went into the Promised Land. Even as God's people, it is very easy for us to want to "go back to Egypt" and revert to the pagan beliefs we held before we became Christians. You will notice this in how, during difficult times, people's fear of witchcraft resurfaces. We easily put our faith in idols, instead of God, when we are faced with scary situations or different forms of suffering.

My neighbour Akinyi heard that her beloved mother-in-law was very sick. She travelled from Nairobi to her rural home in western Kenya to see her. During that trip, Akinyi had an accident involving a motorbike and fractured her leg. My wife drove Akinyi every morning to the hospital.

> We easily put our faith in idols, instead of God, when we are faced with scary situations or different forms of suffering.

About two weeks into Akinyi's treatment, her mother-in-law passed away. Deeply distraught, Akinyi told us she was going to travel back to her rural home to attend the funeral. Her husband told Akinyi that she was not healthy enough to travel. Her legs were still swollen, she was in a great deal of pain, and she could barely walk. My wife and I, and some of our other neighbours, also tried to persuade her not to travel, but she was determined.

Two days later, we received with much shock and dismay, the sad news that Akinyi had passed away. One of our neighbours, a churchgoing woman and a close friend of Akinyi, insisted that this was witchcraft in action. She said Akinyi's recently deceased mother-in-law had supernaturally arranged for Akinyi to leave this world with her.

In another instance, at one of the churches I researched, someone broke into the office and stole a large amount of money from the desk drawer of the church accountant. Upon careful investigations, the church officials came to suspect one of the night guards. They confronted him and informed him that, since this was God's money, the Lord would punish him severely if he did not return the money. He did not seem bothered. A few days later, the church officials threatened to consult a witchdoctor about the incident. The guard was visibly shaken. The following day, the missing amount was mysteriously wired electronically to the phone of the church accountant.

These examples demonstrate that witchcraft is still a source of great fear in the lives of many churchgoing Africans today who are still strongly influenced by an ATR worldview. An automobile accident is not attributed simply to driver carelessness or to mechanical failure, but to a curse. A diviner or witch doctor would be needed to uncover who or what the reason was behind the curse. This would help determine the appropriate ritual for restoring the relationship with the offended spiritual beings that caused the accident. Often these rituals involve libations poured on the ground to appease the spiritual powers and obtain their favour.[56]

The Bible affirms that the unseen spirit world of darkness is real. Christ mentioned the devil and cast out demons. The apostles encountered spiritual enemies and wrote about the reality of evil.

However, the Bible clearly teaches that, although Satan may exercise power through witchcraft, demons, spells, and curses, we have power over all these evil forces through Christ.[57] Christians

> Witchcraft is still a source of great fear in the lives of many churchgoing Africans today.

have been redeemed, forgiven, born again, and delivered from Satan's power by God's work through Christ.[58] Our struggle with the world, the flesh, and the devil springs from our salvation in Jesus Christ. We have the assurance of God's constant presence and the Holy Spirit's indwelling power to guide and sustain us.[59] We can rest assured that we are safe, because God is sovereign and will protect us from all the spiritual dangers we face in this world (Ephesians 6:11-12).

When I was a lecturer at a Bible college, a student asked me to pray with him. His family had moved from one part of the city to another. In their former neighbourhood, his wife's retail shop had provided much needed financial support for her family and his pastoral ministry. In the new neighbourhood, the wife's business floundered. They thought they would get more patrons once they became better-known in the neighbourhood, but several weeks had passed and there was no change. The family was beginning to face financial difficulties.

This student then discovered that their competitor, a more established shop, was owned by a family that was steeped in witchcraft. The student told me this family had consulted witch doctors to ensure that his wife's business would fail. He had been praying about this, but nothing had changed. What was he to do?

"But David," I said to him, "this is a good problem!"

Shocked, he protested, "Teacher, you don't seem to understand the problem!"

"David," I said, "Which is greater, the power of God, or the power of the devil?"

"The power of God, Teacher," he responded feebly, without much conviction.

We agreed to meet regularly to pray together. By the end of that semester, the witchcraft shop was languishing, and David's wife's business was doing as well as it had done in their old neighbourhood. David testified that he had truly witnessed God's faithfulness and power.

The sovereignty of God is the ultimate solution to our fears. As we embrace the content and implications of the gospel in our lives, we find that we enter a richer experience of confidence and assurance as the children of our Father in heaven. Jude's conviction still holds, the conviction that the Lord will protect his people and present them "faultless before the presence of his glory with exceeding joy" through Jesus Christ (Jude 24 KJV).

You Can Trust God

During their wilderness journey, the Israelites needed to believe that God would provide for them when they were in need and protect them against their enemies. Many people can attest to the fact that God is able to deliver and protect believers from demonic influence and attacks and from witchcraft. I personally can attest to this. I hope my experience will encourage you to have faith in God.

In the 1990s I ran an international trading business in Kenya. In this business, one of our trading activities involved importing on a large scale reusable shoes and clothing into the country from Europe and America. Before distributing the shoes to our buyers, we would carefully sort through the goods, which came to us in large gunny bags, to ensure that the shoes were all properly paired, and in good usable condition.

One Sunday evening as I spent time in prayer, the Lord brought Jeremiah 1:8 to my mind: "'Do not be afraid of them, for I am with you and will rescue you,' declares the Lord." I felt burdened to pray strongly for the employees of my business.

The next day, I arrived in the office to find that armed robbers had attacked the company's accountant, Evans. They had stolen from him the large amount of cash that he was going to deposit in the bank that Monday morning. Evans was at a hospital undergoing surgery to remove bullets from his body. Horrified, I rushed to the hospital with a couple of the office staff. We interceded for Evans for several hours. Then the doctors informed us that the surgery had been successful, but they had not been able to remove all the bullets from his body.

A week later, I left home in the morning, but when I was halfway to the office in the city centre, I changed my mind and drove instead to our warehouse in the industrial area. When I arrived at the office a couple of hours later, I discovered two armed robbers had raided my office.

My secretary, Jane, had been present with Evans when he was attacked and shot a week earlier. She recognized the two gunmen who came into the office as being the same ones who had shot Evans. She said this time they asked specifically for me. Not finding me, they stole more money from Jane, roughing her up as well as the office messenger, Edmond. I arrived in the office barely an hour after they had left. If it had not been for my detour to the warehouse, these two dangerous men would probably have found me in the office and shot me to death.

I locked the office door and prayed with Jane and Edmond, saying, "Dear Lord, thank you for preserving our lives. We forgive these two dangerous men for the harm they have inflicted on us. We ask that you meet with them and bring them to repentance so that they can stop going around hurting others."

A few days later, Jane saw the two dangerous men on the TV evening news. Apparently, they had attacked one of the distributors of our company's merchandise in one of the city's sprawling markets. As they tried to get away with the money they had taken from this hapless lady, they ran into a team of fully armed policemen who shot them both to death on the spot.

Every evening after work, I would go with a few other employees from the office to visit and pray for Evans in the hospital. One evening, I arrived after the others had left. I stood by Evans's bedside, not sure what to do, since he was still in a semi-conscious state. I placed my hand on his belly and prayed briefly for his recovery, and then I left.

When Evans regained full consciousness a few days later, he said to me, "Sir, do you remember placing your hands on my belly and praying for me a few days ago?" Despite not being fully conscious, he said he recognized my voice, as if from a far place, as I spoke to the nurses in his hospital ward that evening. "I was in so much pain that I was asking the Lord to take me home, just to end the pain. However, as soon as you laid your hand on my belly and prayed, the pain immediately disappeared and it has not come back!"

I was shocked! *My prayer, my hand? Wow!* We both gave thanks to God for this miracle of healing that was the result of a few seconds of prayer on my part.

While Evans continued to recover, I received a call from our European supplier. He had shipped shoes to another of his clients in Nairobi who was having difficulty selling them. He asked me to see if I could sell them. As was our practice, we paired the shoes in our warehouse, certified their condition, and sold the shoes in few days without any difficulty at all. I then called our European supplier to inform him that I was going to transfer the funds to him. To my utter astonishment, he asked me to keep the money. Without knowing anything about our predicament, the supplier had given us more money than we had lost to the two gunmen!

Later, I discovered that one of our competitors in the industry, very upset that she was losing her long-time customers on account of our better products, had been behind the attempt to

By simple prayer, the Lord protected my staff and me from real danger.

murder me and hurt our business. I realized why, that Sunday evening in prayer, the Lord had given me his promise of protection from Jeremiah 1:8.

If I had not known better, I would easily have attributed the entire experience to witchcraft and probably sought the aid of witch doctors. But we put our faith in God. By the simple process of regularly spending time in prayer, the Lord protected my staff and me from real danger. Evans recovered fully. Although he still walks with a limp to this day, that experience of God's deliverance so marked his life that he is now pastoring a large church in one of the growing suburbs on the outskirts of Nairobi.

This experience, and many others I can testify to over the years, enable me to testify to the truth of Christ's words, "But seek first his kingdom and his righteousness, and all these things will be given to you as well. Therefore do not worry about tomorrow, for tomorrow will worry about itself. Each day has enough trouble of its own" (Matthew 6:33-34).

The unavoidable alternative to a life of faith in God is a life that is frequently overshadowed by fear, anxiety, depression, and worry, especially during times of crisis, such as the Israelites experienced in the wilderness because of their unbelief.

Many Christians in Africa testify that when they submitted their lives to Christ, they moved from their earlier fear of evil spirits to the peace that comes from a relationship with God through Christ. Isaiah 26:3 says of God, "You will keep in perfect peace those whose minds are steadfast, because they trust in you."

> The unavoidable alternative to a life of faith in God is a life that is frequently overshadowed by fear.

Have Faith

Many churches today teach that God's blessing to us depends on how much tithes and offering we bring to our pastors or on how much faith we have. People are thus being led away from true faith in God to unbiblical ideas influenced by an ATR worldview. Jude would have us remember that God harshly judged the Israelites, and they forfeited God's blessing, on account of such unbelief. Like many Africans today, although they had left Egypt, the paganism of Egypt was still in them.

The gospel truth, however, is that our blessing comes from our faith in God's promise to meet the needs of his people based on the finished work of Christ for us on the cross. Spiritually, through the gospel, God blesses us with his redemption and transformation. Materially, we can trust that "If God didn't hesitate to put everything on the line for us, embracing our condition and exposing himself to the worst by sending his own Son, is there anything else he wouldn't gladly and freely do for us?" (Romans 8:32, MSG).

Our faith in God connects us to the fundamental realities of the promises of God in the gospel (Hebrews 4:1-3). Our faith in God enables us to trust in God's goodness demonstrated to us in the death of Jesus Christ. Our faith in God can be our shield of confidence that will keep us secure in this world until the day we will finally pass through the gates of death into life that will last for ever.

Questions for Reflection and Discussion

1. What are some examples of having faith in faith itself, in offerings, in special objects, or in special words? What is the difference between this and trusting God?

2. Can you share a story of how you have seen false teaching hurt people or even shipwreck their faith?

3. In Numbers 13 and 14, why were the Israelites afraid in the wilderness and when the spies reported on the land of Canaan? Why was their response mistaken?

4. Can you describe a time in your life when God's power triumphed over the powers of darkness?

Abundance

CHAPTER 6
PROSPERITY, GREED, AND MONEY

Woe to them! They have taken the way of Cain;
they have rushed for profit into Balaam's error;
they have been destroyed in Korah's rebellion (Jude 11).

I drove into the sprawling church compound of one of the very large new churches in an upmarket suburb of the capital city. An hour into the Overcomer's Hour Wednesday morning service, there were hardly any parking spaces left in the huge parking lot. I was attending the service before my appointment with the senior pastor, who had kindly agreed to meet with me as part of my doctoral research and to introduce me to some of the church's other pastors.

I walked up to the large, modern church hall. A large poster in the corridor advertised anointed olive oil, handkerchiefs, and holy water, and a wide variety of other consecrated items. In the middle of the working week, the church hall was packed, mostly with young women. Next to me sat a 26-year-old single mother who occasionally checked on her six-month old baby, sleeping on a mat at the back of the hall.

A young man in the pulpit led the prayer sessions. He called for the congregants to bind all evil forces, to boldly declare their breakthroughs, to take hold of their destiny. "This is your season of victory! There is power for abundance here today!" The young woman sitting next to me took in every word.

Then he called the audience to sow their seeds. "Your seed is your claim to your increase!" The young woman ran forward.

Towards the end of the service the founder stepped into the pulpit. "Praise the Lord!"

"Hallelujah!" the congregation replied.

He waved a large bunch of keys above his head, "Do you see these keys?" he said three times.

"Yes!" the audience replied each time.

"We are going to open some doors and close some doors!" The young woman next to me yelled and jumped up and down.

The founder said, "Next week, make sure you bring many keys with you. We will be opening doors and closing doors. All the doors that should be open will be opened and every door that should be shut will be shut. Hallelujah!" There was more singing and another offering where more people sowed their seeds.

At the end of the service, I struck up a conversation with the young woman next to me. She was a hairdresser. She never missed these midweek services. Life was hard, she said, but she was sure her breakthrough was on the way. "I'll bring my keys next week!" she said brightly.

Sowing Seeds

An integral part of the prosperity doctrine is the seed-faith principle. This is the belief that tithes and offerings are the seeds of faith that one is required to plant to reap rewards from God, rewards such as untold wealth and unfailing health. This principle is taken from a misinterpretation of 2 Corinthians 9:6, "Remember this: Whoever sows sparingly will also reap sparingly, and whoever sows generously will also reap generously." The verse is often used in conjunction with 2 Corinthians 8:9, "For you know the grace of our Lord Jesus Christ, that though he was rich, yet for your sake he became poor, so that you through his poverty, might become rich."

Many preachers today use these two passages in 2 Corinthians to teach that God wants Christians to be materially rich, and that God will bless Christians with wealth if they generously pay their tithes and offerings to the church. The historical, cultural, and literary contexts of these verses, however, yield a very different meaning.

Acts 11:27-30 explains the context of Paul's statements in 2 Corinthians. A prophet had predicted a severe famine would affect the Roman world. The Gentile Christians in Antioch decided to give relief to the largely Jewish mother church in Judea. Paul facilitated this collection from the network of Gentile churches he had planted across the Roman province of Asia, sending representatives to Corinth and Galatia to help gather the donations (1 Corinthians 16:1-4, and 2 Corinthians 8:6 and 10). He didn't want to ask the poor Macedonian church to contribute, but even they were eager to participate (2 Corinthians 8:1-5). Various Asian churches participated in this collection and sent delegates with Paul to Jerusalem (Acts 20:4; 21:17-19; 1 Corinthians 16:1-4).

So, when he spoke about sowing and reaping, Paul was not encouraging the Corinthian Christians to give towards his own ministry. In fact, he had already specifically told the Corinthians that he preached the gospel free of charge instead of requesting support from his listeners (1 Corinthians 9:18). He was encouraging them to be generous towards their fellow believers in Judea who were at risk of going hungry.

Because Jesus gave up everything for their salvation, they should respond in gratitude. They should become like Christ, imitating his sacrificial generosity.

When Paul used Christ's example of becoming poor so that they might become rich, he wasn't telling them that Christ died so they could be materially wealthy. Anyone could see from Paul's life that following Jesus didn't make you wealthy. Paul had just reminded them earlier in his letter how he had been hungry, beaten, and poor (2 Corinthians 6:4-10). Jesus also talked about wealth as a barrier to accepting the gospel: how it is harder for a rich man to enter the Kingdom of God than for a camel to pass through the hole in a needle, and how the rich young ruler refused to become a disciple because he didn't want to give his possessions to the poor (Luke 18:18-25).

Paul could not have been motivating the Corinthians with greed. Instead, he was pointing them to the gospel as their motivation to give generously. Christ had left the glory of the Trinity to become a human being and die a criminal's death. As a result, we have the rich inheritance of eternal life with God (Titus 3:7). Paul was exhorting the Corinthian Christians that, because Jesus gave up everything for their salvation, they should respond in gratitude. They should become like Christ, imitating his sacrificial generosity.[60]

Paul does suggest that God will bless them for their generosity, using the language of sowing and reaping. But look at the context:

> Remember this: whoever sows sparingly will also reap sparingly, and whoever sows generously will also reap generously ... And God is able to bless you abundantly, *so that* in all things at all

times, having all that you need, you will abound in every good work. As it is written:

'They have freely scattered their gifts *to the poor*;
their righteousness endures for ever.'

Now he who supplies seed to the sower and bread for food will also supply and increase your store of seed and will enlarge the harvest of your righteousness. You will be enriched in every way *so that* you can be generous on every occasion, and through us your generosity will result in thanksgiving to God (2 Corinthians 9:6, 8-11, emphasis mine).

First of all, the gifts are given to the poor. Second, God meets people's needs and blesses them so that they can do abundant good deeds of generosity, which will result in people praising God.

We see an example of the early church living this out in the book of Acts, when the believers met regularly in Jerusalem for prayer, fellowship, and teaching:

All the believers were together and had everything in common. They sold property and possessions to give to anyone who had need. Every day they continued to meet together in the temple courts. They broke bread in their homes and ate together with glad and sincere hearts, praising God and enjoying the favour of all the people. And the Lord added to their number daily those who were being saved (Acts 2:44-47).

The generosity of the believers providing for the needy, brought praise to God, and drew people to Christ.

However, preachers and teachers in many churches today misuse these principles to make unending demands for tithes and offerings.

In a four-day African church conference, a preacher urged those attending "to sell cars, houses and property and close bank accounts, before the fundraising on Sunday, and give to the church."[61] It is true that we see people in the early church selling their houses and land for the church. But, as in Paul's letter to the Corinthians, it was so that the poor and needy people among them would be cared for:

> All the believers were one in heart and mind. No one claimed that any of their possessions was their own, but they shared everything they had . . . *there was no needy person among them*. For from time to time those who owned land or houses sold them, brought the money from the sales and put it at the apostles' feet, and it was distributed *to anyone who had need* (Acts 4:32-35, emphasis mine).

Another important distinction is that the members of the church in the book of Acts were not giving in order to get blessings. They were giving because God had already abundantly blessed them in Christ. They gave because they were a united community and they wanted to support what God was doing among them. It is true that if we belong to a local congregation, we should support the work of that congregation, both in terms of giving towards the financial support of the clergy and the various ministries of the church (Galatians 6:6). However, there is a difference between supporting versus being taken advantage of by church leaders. The false teachers in Jude used loud and boastful words to flatter those among his readers on whom they depended financially for their prosperous living (Jude 16).

From looking at these verses within the context of the letters to the Corinthians and the rest of the New Testament, we see that these verses should not be used by church leaders to encourage poor people to give towards their own ministry. It should be used to

encourage giving to the poor. People should give, not to get more money, but with a cheerful heart. They should be motivated by gratitude for Christ's sacrifice to be generous like him, so that God receives praise and honour.

Diviners in the Church

Prosperity preachers using the seed faith principle give people the wrong motivation for giving. They claim churchgoers must make generous financial contributions to the church to receive material blessings from God. One prominent African prosperity preacher declared in a sermon that, "God blesses us according to our deposits. If you haven't deposited anything, you have no right to ask for anything" and then went on to declare that people should give to the church "so the God of Abraham, Isaac, and Jacob will meet all your needs."[62]

In ATR culture, Africans are used to paying diviners and religious specialists for their services.

In return, many of these churches and their leaders promise to make their church members prosperous with cars, houses, a husband or wife, physical health, and professional success. One of the churches I researched was completing the construction of their church building, a building that included seating for several thousand worshippers. In the Sunday service that I attended, the pastor said, "We need to install the windows. If you only pay for a window, you will find God will bless you with a house. You will be surprised that you have only contributed for a window and God will give you a car. If you visit other churches and they pass around an offering bag, you can contribute a small amount. But the bulk of your money should come here, where you are members." The windows each cost about $200, which is a typical monthly salary for a middle-class professional such as a teacher or an office worker.

In another church I researched, I came across a lay leader who had a strong background in corporate finance. One of the young preachers at the church was being groomed by the founding pastor and he had caught on to the techniques of obtaining money from church members very quickly. The lay leader told me this young preacher would often ask for money from him. Even though he felt uncomfortable, he gave in time and time again because the young preacher insisted that if he didn't give the money to the man of God, he would miss God's blessing. As he told me this story, he was close to tears because of how harassed he felt.

In ATR culture, Africans are used to paying diviners and religious specialists for their services. With an ATR worldview, if you want to be healed or your crops to prosper or your husband to love you, you will need to bring a chicken or some form of payment in exchange for your blessing. This cause-and-effect payment for services attitude has crept into the church by promising people blessings for their donations.

Another similarity is that in ATR, diviners often give the person a potion, an object, or a ritual to perform to produce the results they desire. In the church I visited, they sold anointing oil and holy water as the potions, and the preacher asked people to bring keys to the service to perform a ritual together that would unlock blessings. This comparison may seem harsh, but consider Paul, who warned that false doctrines spiritually originate from deceiving spirits and demons (1 Timothy 4:1).

Jude compares the false teachers of his day to a diviner as well. In verse 11, Jude says the false teachers "have rushed for profit into Balaam's error". Balaam was a diviner (Joshua 13:22) with an international reputation. Numbers 22–25 tells the story of how Balak, the king of Moab, sent messengers all the way to Balaam's homeland to hire him to curse Israel. The Lord actually spoke to

Balaam, warning him not to go, and finally saying that if he went, he must say nothing except the Lord's message. Balak prepared sacrifices three times, but each time Balaam blessed Israel instead of cursing them. Of course, Balak refused to pay Balaam for blessing his enemies.

If Balaam, a diviner who desperately wanted to resist God's Word, was forced to bless Israel even though it meant not being paid, why should we have to pay pastors, who claim to speak God's Word, in order to receive whatever blessings God already wants to give us? How can a godless diviner give free blessings from God and pastors insist on payment?

The Idolatry of Money

Balaam realized God would only punish Israel if they disobeyed, so he "taught Balak to entice the Israelites to sin so that they ate food sacrificed to idols and committed sexual immorality" (Revelation 2:14). Immediately after Balaam went home, women from Moab, Balak's people, seduced Israelite men into sexual immorality, and invited them to sacrifice to their god, Baal. The Lord punished them for their idolatry, sending a plague that killed 24,000 people (Numbers 25). Later, the Israelites fought against these people, killing Balaam and the women who had seduced Israel (Numbers 31:8, 15-18).

Both Jude and 2 Peter compare Balaam to the false teachers they write against. Second Peter 2:15 says because Balaam "loved the wages of wickedness", he was determined to go to Balak, even after the Lord told him he wouldn't be able to curse them. Jude says they have "rushed for profit into Balaam's error". Paul also wrote against false teachers "who have been robbed of the truth and who think that godliness is a means to financial gain" (1 Timothy 6:5). The truth is that these false

> When we consider our lives hardly worth living without something, that thing has become an idol.

teachers are motivated by sheer greed for financial gain. If there is a promise of payment, they would be willing to encourage immorality and idolatry and to contradict the Word of the Lord. During my doctoral research, for example, I heard stories from church members of pastors who take large offerings from known drug dealers and pray for their illegal drug smuggling enterprises. It is not an exaggeration to say that in some churches today, we see leaders willing to say whatever will finance their ministries and lifestyles, even if it means encouraging people in the idolatry of money.

> We use the idols of status, success, money, power, wealth, and pleasure as fig leaves to cover our inner sense of shame in our desperate search for meaning and purpose in our lives.

We make something an idol when it becomes more important to us than God. Our idol absorbs our hearts and imagination. We feel our idol will give our lives meaning, will make us significant, and will give us security or meet our needs.[63] We can put our trust in ATR or other religious specialists, but we can also make idols of work, marriage, wealth, positions, or ministries. When we consider our lives hardly worth living without something, that thing has become an idol.

When Adam and Eve broke their relationship with God, they found themselves adrift from the security of faith in God. They used fig leaves to cover up their shame and confusion. Like our first parents, we use the idols of status, success, money, power, wealth, and pleasure as fig leaves. We use them to cover our inner sense of shame in our desperate search for meaning and purpose in our lives.

For many people, money is an idol. When we have a lot of money, we falsely feel in control of our lives and independent from God. Money makes us feel safe, because we can use it to get food, clothing, and shelter. Without money, we feel anxious, frightened, and depressed.

Money makes us feel significant. We see ourselves as raised above the common people, earning us societal approval and respect. We envy and honour people with much money, and we pity and look down on people without money. Money gives us power and opens doors for us. Poverty makes us feel weak and inadequate, but money delivers us from this feeling. Poverty comes with sickness, adversity, and a loss of social status. The Ghanaian Pentecostal Bible scholar, Joseph Quayesi-Amakye, explains that this is the rationale behind churches which focus on economic empowerment:

> Wealth affirms, dominates, controls and commands respect . . . It commands submission and audience, refines status and elicits fear. The rich and wealthy are adored and are served at their beckon. Young or old, the wealthy command authority and power. We live in a world of power and the powerful are the rulers; the poor have no place in this world of power.[64]

Because people believe money can do all this for them, they will steal, kill, and lie to get money at all costs. For instance, governments around the world raised large amounts of relief funds in 2020 to provide care and support to their populations during the Covid-19 pandemic. In Kenya, during the early months of the pandemic, the media reported that government officials were colluding with shadowy businessmen to defraud the country and had suddenly become *pandemic billionaires.* Such callousness and greed while people were sick and dying revealed these people had made money their idol.

To be clear, money, in and of itself, is a good thing if we allow it to have its God-intended place in our lives as a store of value, a measure of wealth, and a means of exchange in trade. But as sinful humans, we easily make money the ultimate thing in our lives and allow it to replace God as the source of our meaning, our purpose, and our sense of fulfilment. It is not money in and of itself but greed (the love of money) that is dangerous, as Paul warned:

> Those who want to get rich fall into temptation and a trap and into many foolish and harmful desires that plunge people into ruin and destruction. For the love of money is a root of all kinds of evil. Some people, eager for money, have wandered from the faith and pierced themselves with many griefs (1 Timothy 6:9-10).

This is why Paul urged his readers to turn away from evil desires and "greed, which is idolatry" (Colossians 3:5).

Only God is Worthy of Our Worship

The problem with making money an idol is that it cannot do what only God can do.

Only God can save us, although we are tempted to look to money for security. The first of the Ten Commandments said, "You shall have no other gods before me." But before God gave them this first commandment, he first said, "I am the Lord your God, who brought you out of Egypt, out of the land of slavery" (Exodus 20:3, 2). God reminded the Israelites how he had supernaturally delivered them from bondage and that he would adequately provide for them, making idolatry unnecessary.

The apostles echo this theme when they warn Christians to avoid idolatry because God is the one who has delivered them from slavery to sin (1 John 5:21; 1 Corinthians 10:14). Paul reminds Christians that Christ became a living sacrifice for us. This is our motivation to worship the one God by offering ourselves as a living sacrifice, or in other words, obeying God with our whole lives (Romans 12:1-2).

Only God lasts for ever. But money can be here today and gone tomorrow.

Peter reminds us that "it was not with perishable things such as silver or gold that you were redeemed . . . but with the precious blood of Christ" (1 Peter 1:18-19). Christ suffered for our sins to bring us to God – not gold (1 Peter 3:18), so we must obey him as Lord (1 Peter 1:2).

Only God lasts for ever, so it is only God and our relationship with him that we cannot lose, for all eternity. But money can be here today and gone tomorrow. "Cast but a glance at riches, and they are gone, for they will surely sprout wings and fly off to the sky like an eagle" (Proverbs 23:5). Jesus calls wealth "deceitful"; its promises cannot be trusted (Matthew 13:22).

When a man approached Jesus with concern that he wasn't getting his fair share of the inheritance, Jesus warned him, "Watch out! Be on your guard against all kinds of greed; life does not consist in an abundance of possessions" (Luke 12:15). Then he told a parable about a man who built bigger barns to store his abundant harvest – only for God to end his life that same night.

Jesus was showing that in the end money will fail us. We will lose anything that we trust in more than God. This is why Christ invites us to a better investment, "Sell your possessions and give to the poor. Provide purses for yourselves that will not wear out, a treasure in heaven that will never fail, where no thief comes near and no moth destroys. For where your treasure is, there your heart will be also" (Luke 12:33-34).

Jesus told this parable after he had already set off for Jerusalem, where he knew he would be crucified. Jesus would live out this truth by giving up all his heavenly glory, honour, and wealth so that we could have God's goodness of salvation in this world and eternal life in the world to come.

Only God can meet our needs, which is another reason we should trust God instead of money. When the Lord told the Israelites, "You shall have no other gods" and reminded them of his deliverance in Egypt, God was actually promising them that they wouldn't need any other gods because he would provide for them. For 40 long years, in miracle after miracle, the Lord faithfully and very adequately provided for Israel in the wilderness, giving them water, food, clothing, direction, protection, and leadership.

As I have already explained above, I used to run a business that imported shoes and clothes into Kenya from Europe and America. We would carefully sort through the gunny sacks of shoes, to pair them up and ensure they were in good usable condition. In July 1998, the business faced a cash flow crisis. I could see we would not have enough money to pay our 20 employees at the end of the month. I considered applying for an overdraft from our bank. As I sat in my office praying about this situation, the Lord asked me to trust him with this financial crisis, and I suddenly felt peace.

When the staff went on their lunch break, I walked through the quiet warehouse. Something bright yellow caught my eye. It was rolled up paper, sticking out from one of the shoes on the floor. Inside this paper was a wad of brand-new banknotes of a European currency – more than enough to meet our financial crisis. I was shocked. The workers had been working on the shoes all morning. How could they have missed this, unless it had not been there? This miracle taught me to trust God to provide.

> The church has its head, Christ, in heaven while its feet and hands, who are Christians, perform God's will and work physically here on earth.

Contentment with God's provision helps us avoid falling into the trap of greed. When Paul warned against the false teachers who loved money and pursued godliness as a means to financial gain, he gave Timothy some advice for how to avoid their trap: "But godliness with contentment is great gain. For we brought nothing into the world, and we can take nothing out of it. But if we have food and clothing, we will be content with that" (1 Timothy 6:6-8). Paul advised rich Christians not "to put their hope in wealth, which is so uncertain, but to put their hope in God, who richly provides us with everything for our enjoyment" (1 Timothy 6:17).

> Our work is a way we partner with God in his love and care for the world.

Working Your Way Out of Poverty

The young woman who sat next to me at the Overcomer's Hour service had left her work as a hairdresser to attend. Although the services were on Wednesday mornings, she had made this a habit because the prosperity doctrine promised her magical quick riches from "sowing seed." Her church had not taught her to see any connection between her relationship with her Lord and her work.

God works. He worked for six days to create the universe. After seeing God deliver his people from Egypt and guide them through the wilderness, Moses prayed, "Who can do the deeds and mighty works you do?" (Deuteronomy 3:24). Jesus worked as a carpenter.[65] As he went about his earthly ministry, Jesus said, "My Father is always at his work to this very day, and I too am working" (John 5:17). His Father in heaven was working to redeem and transform people's lives through the ministry of Christ and his disciples.

Christians from every background together make up the church, also called *the body of Christ* (1 Corinthians 12:13). Our brains in our heads direct our bodies. Similarly, Christ, as the head of the church, directs us to fulfil his redemptive purposes in this world, through the Holy Spirit who dwells in us. The resurrected and living Lord Jesus, exalted and seated at the right hand of the Father in heaven, is connected to his body, the church, here on earth. The church, in other words, has its head, Christ, in heaven while its feet and hands, who are Christians, perform God's will and work physically here on earth. The Lord has distributed different spiritual gifts to the members of his body so that, as each member plays his part, the church can grow into spiritual maturity (1 Corinthians 12; Ephesians 4:11-16).

God also equips all people with talents and gifts for the material work of building up the human community.[66] Whether as business people, lawyers, teachers, healthcare workers, merchants, carpenters, or farmers, our work is a way we partner with God in his love and care for the world. He works through us, which gives our work new meaning and purpose. As Psalm 127:1 says, "Unless the Lord builds the house, the builders labour in vain." The new life we receive in Christ can change our work from frustrating, self-dependent toil to restful God-dependent trust.

Poverty and material deprivation are results of the Fall that do not honour God in any way. But God brings us out of poverty and blesses us by meeting our material needs through our honest, God-enabled, hard work. When God's people do work that is enabled by God and depends on him, God blesses it and uses it to display his glory and his material sufficiency in their lives.

> God brings us out of poverty and blesses us by meeting our material needs through our honest, God-enabled, hard work.

The young hairdresser who sat next to me that Wednesday morning needed to know that God was inviting her to partner with Christ, our Lord, in both his material and spiritual work in the world. God wanted her to work hard and with careful planning. God wanted her to trust him for fruitfulness in the face of "self-denial, . . . weakness and apparent failure, . . . hard thought, . . . and steady faithfulness" in the tiring and often boring routines of our work.[67]

Conclusion

When Jude compares the false teachers to Balaam, he shows that they would disobey God to get money. We see something similar today. The greed we see displayed by some church leaders demonstrates that they have made money an idol. Their teaching and lifestyle encourage their followers to do the same. The prosperity doctrine teaches that God wants his children to be wealthy and financially successful and happy. It teaches people to look to money, health, and material success to give them their sense of hope, meaning, purpose, significance, and security in their lives. Such teaching would have us trust in these idols, instead of trusting in God based on what Christ has done for us.

> The gospel presents Christ, who died on our behalf, as the ultimate giver.

But the gospel helps to free us from idolatry. We learn that the number of possessions we own isn't what defines our lives (Luke 12:14-21). The gospel presents Christ, who died on our behalf, as the ultimate giver. At infinite cost, he gave up everything to give us himself. This truth gives us a sense of the long-term security and joy we have in Christ. It enables us not to hoard, but rather to give away our wealth. It enables us to work alongside God in trust and diligence to provide for ourselves and to bless others.

Questions for Reflection and Discussion

1. What is the difference between what Paul meant by sowing seeds and reaping and how we misuse this idea today?

2. What was your reaction to the comparison between Balaam and false teachers today?

3. In what ways may money be an inadvertent idol in your life? In what ways can the gospel help you to dethrone this idol from your life?

4. In what ways do you see yourself partnering with God, through your work, in his care for his world?

CHAPTER 7

SELFISH SHEPHERDS AND FALSE HOPE

These people are blemishes at your love feasts, eating with
you without the slightest qualm – shepherds who feed only
themselves. They are clouds without rain, blown along by the
wind; autumn trees, without fruit and uprooted – twice dead.
They are wild waves of the sea, foaming up their shame;
wandering stars, for whom blackest darkness
has been reserved for ever (Jude 12-13).

Michael was born and raised in a Roman Catholic church. As a teenager, he drifted away from the church. In his 20s, he experienced three carjackings in Nairobi. He knew he could have lost his life, and he marvelled that his life was spared all three times. He felt a supernatural nudge about God's love for him.

On a visit to the UK, he was invited to attend a church service. During the service, after a long session of loud singing, everyone in

What would happen to their wealth if church members stopped paying the tithes and offerings and sowing their financial seeds that these leaders repeatedly demanded from them?

the church suddenly began to pray loudly in unintelligible words, some with arms raised up in the air. Having grown up in the Catholic church, this experience put Michael off. For several years, he did not even attend any church at all.

One morning, however, in Nairobi, as he listened to an evangelist preaching the gospel on TV, Michael came powerfully under the conviction of the Holy Spirit. He surrendered his life to Christ. He joined a local church and he began to grow spiritually. He joined a Bible study group with other young people.

As Michael's church continued to grow numerically, he observed several disturbing trends in the church leadership. He noticed that a great emphasis was placed on tithes and offerings. Michael began to date a female church member who informed him that one of the married church leaders was consistently making sexual advances to her.

Michael considered moving to a different church, but in the churches he visited, he kept finding a similar emphasis on tithes and offerings and sowing seeds. Michael saw that the promises of material affluence made by church leaders were often not fulfilled in the real lives of church members, but the leaders were wealthy. He wondered what would happen to their wealth if church members stopped paying the tithes and offerings and sowing their financial seeds that these leaders repeatedly demanded from them.

Shepherds Who Feed Themselves

The Bible often uses the word *shepherd* as a metaphor for spiritual leaders such as Moses (Numbers 27:16-17), David (2 Samuel 5:2), or Jesus (John 10:15-17; 1 Peter 2:25). Jude's expression, "shepherds who feed only themselves," refers to Ezekiel 34, where Ezekiel prophesies against Israel's corrupt spiritual and political leaders:

> "This is what the Sovereign Lord says: woe to you shepherds of Israel who only take care of yourselves! Should not shepherds take care of the flock? You eat the curds, clothe yourselves with the wool and slaughter the choice animals, but you do not take care of the flock" (Ezekiel 34:2-3).

Jude was warning his readers that their spiritual leaders were like the greedy and selfish shepherds of Ezekiel 34. God had entrusted his people to their care, but the shepherds exploited them to clothe and feed themselves. The prosperity doctrine being preached in many African churches today also seems to enrich only the church leaders who, like these men in Jude's epistle, are just interested in feeding themselves.[68] In countries where most people earn less than 200 dollars a month, many prosperity preachers are known to earn thousands of dollars every month.

A young Ghanaian pastor was pickpocketed while visiting Nairobi and lost his wallet. He was stranded in a foreign city. As he walked the streets of the city wondering from where he could obtain help, he came upon a large Pentecostal church. As a Pentecostal pastor himself, he walked into this church and told his story to one of the pastors of this church.

> The prosperity doctrine seems to enrich only the church leaders who, like these men in Jude's epistle, are just interested in feeding themselves.

Without offering any help at all, the Kenyan pastor inexplicably drove the Ghanaian pastor to the nearest police station and left him there. The Ghanaian pastor languished for several days in the cells of this police station, not knowing what to do.

Eventually a visitor to the police station heard about his fate and gave him my telephone number. Through our intervention, the pastor was released from the police station, we got in touch with his relatives in Ghana, and eventually he made his way back home.

The wealthy prosperity preachers obtain the hard-earned money of financially struggling church members. They use it to erect costly church buildings and furnish plush office suites. They are chauffeured around in brand-new four-wheel-drive vehicles. They build personal financial empires and use their followers' tithes and offerings to finance their lavish lifestyles. Then, they hold up their riches as evidence of the validity of their doctrine. One African prosperity preacher recently "opened his house and wardrobe to a local TV station to film his luxurious estate and expensive cars."[69] This reminds us of Jude's accusation that the false teachers only followed their own evil desires, boasting about themselves, and flattering those among his readers on whom they depended financially for their prosperous living (Jude 16).

If the leaders of our new growing African churches begin to preach the gospel and to live by its implications, they will affirm in their own experience that a definite blessing of the gospel is that God's work done God's way will always receive God's adequate financial support. They will be pleasantly surprised to discover that, as they turn away from depending on teaching that has departed from the gospel to build their personal church kingdoms, they will be joining God to build his enduring Kingdom in this world. They will thus discover that there is no need for them to coerce money from churchgoers through the preaching of the false prosperity doctrine, because as Christ promised in Matthew 6:33, everyone

The Lord has consistently lived up to his promise to meet our needs.

who seeks first the Kingdom of God will find that God will gladly and adequately provide for all their legitimate needs.

Again, I can personally testify to the truth of this in my own experience. I remember how frightened and reluctant I was when, many years ago, the Lord made it very clear to me that he wanted me to leave the business world and go into full-time ministry, assuring me that he would be responsible for meeting the needs of myself and my family. Over the years I can say that although this hasn't been easy, as we continue to learn to do his work his way, in many ways, the Lord has consistently lived up to his promise to meet our needs. A recent experience can illustrate this.

My daughter's school fees in the US were due before the end of 2019, and my wife and I prayed that God would provide. We attended a Christmas Day luncheon for the members of the small church that we had planted with an American missionary couple to reach the unchurched and unreached people in an affluent Nairobi suburb. One church member called my wife aside and told her that the Lord had specifically instructed her to give a certain sum of money to my wife and me. The gift was enough to pay our daughter's fees on time, plus enough to leave us some money to financially cushion us during the Covid-19 pandemic, which started a few months later.

This is just one of many, many times when the Lord has proven to my wife and me that our heavenly Father knows what we need, and as we seek first his Kingdom, he is more than willing and able to meet all our needs just when we need him to do so (Matthew 6:33).

Shepherds Who Don't Care for the Flock

Ezekiel continues to prophesy against the spiritual leaders:

> You have not strengthened the weak or healed those who are ill
> or bound up the injured. You have not brought back the strays
> or searched for the lost. You have ruled them harshly and
> brutally. So they were scattered because there was no shepherd,

and when they were scattered they became food for all the wild
animals (Ezekiel 34:4-5).

These "shepherds who feed only themselves" refused to care for the
weak, sick, vulnerable, and lost. If there was no profit for them, they
were not concerned if the sheep were attacked and died.

In the 1990s I served on the advisory board of a ministry based in
Kenya that focuses on evangelism to Muslims. When Muslims come
to Christ, they face hostility from their families and communities.
They desperately need to find acceptance in a new, loving, supportive
community of Christians. However, when we approached local
churches for support and a spiritual home for these new converts,
the church leaders shied away in suspicion and resentment. They
frequently informed us they were more focused on tending to the
needs of their church members. We were offering them an opportunity
to disciple new converts, but to our dismay, they turned it down.
Like the shepherds in Ezekiel, they did not have a heart for missions
or for the lost.

One of the churches I visited during my doctoral research is located
very close to a beach in Accra. A very heavy rainfall destroyed the
flimsy makeshift homes of the squatters who lived on this beach. The
people became homeless. Some of the church members wanted to
minister to these poor people by offering them food, clothing, and
basic materials to rebuild their destroyed dwellings. They brought
their request to the church. The church leadership refused, saying that
the church did not need to have these people join the church because
they could not be counted on to bring in any tithes and offerings.

At a large church in Nairobi, I preached a four-part sermon series
on what giving is, and why, how, and when we should give. Several
church members told me that although the teaching was helpful,
they still didn't want to give because the church leaders didn't care

for needy widows and orphans in their midst. They said the leaders were more interested in spending money on luxury cars and on costly sound equipment.

If we see someone who needs clothes and daily food and we do nothing about it, James says our faith is dead (James 2:14-17). James 2:13 then tells us that, "Judgment without mercy will be shown to anyone who has not been merciful." The lack of mercy in our attitudes and actions towards others reveal that, in our hearts, we are strangers to the saving mercy and grace of God embodied in the gospel of Jesus Christ. Jude's appeal to his readers to show mercy to those who require mercy is then simply lost on us.

Jesus's mission included ministry to the poor, the captives, the blind, and the oppressed (Luke 4:14-30). Likewise, as the church, we show God's love both through evangelism and social ministry; sometimes people's hunger or need is so pressing that they wouldn't be able to hear the gospel if we shared it with them.[70] When the church cares for those in need, when it works for the transformation of social and institutional injustice, the church fulfils its call to be God's means of transforming the world through the full implications of the gospel.[71]

> False teachers offer no real spiritual value or benefit. Like clouds, these men and their teaching will eventually be blown away by the wind.

Empty Words

Jude says the false teachers "are clouds without rain, blown along by the wind". When we see clouds, we expect life-giving rain. But these clouds disappoint. When people come to church, they expect life-giving teaching, but the false teachers offer no real spiritual value or benefit. Like clouds, these men and their teaching will eventually be blown away by the wind.

The teachers are like "autumn trees without fruit and uprooted – twice dead." In autumn one expects harvest, just as people expect fruit and spiritual nourishment from teachers. But they produce no fruit. They fulfil no purpose of eternal value. Fruitless trees are only worthy of being cut down (Matthew 3:10; Luke 3:9).

In Mark 11, Christ encountered a fig tree that should have fruited by then, but it had not. So, he cursed it and it died. Right after cursing the fig tree, Christ went into the Temple and cleared the Temple. By cursing the fig tree, Christ was demonstrating a parable of the clearing of the Temple. The fig tree had leaves and looked luxurious, but there was no fruit. The same was true of the Temple, where there was a great deal of loud and busy religious activity, but no real spiritual fruit.

We find in many of our growing churches in Africa today, a lot of noise, music, dancing, and prayer meetings. Some of our nations are "Christian nations" with impressive church attendance records. But, as people often complain, our nations are no less corrupt than "non-Christian nations". Where is the character change in churchgoers that demonstrates the fruit of the Spirit and draws others to Christ? How would Christ respond today to our churches if he were to suddenly show up in our midst? I fear Christ would dismiss our empty religious activity the same way that he dismissed the fig tree and the Temple.[72]

Jude compares the false teachers to "wild waves of the sea, foaming up their shame", waves that leave nothing but debris and destruction in their wake. Jude goes on to describe them as "wandering stars, for whom blackest darkness has been reserved for ever". Their temporary charisma is like a shooting

> How would Christ respond today to our churches if he were to suddenly show up in our midst? I fear Christ would dismiss our empty religious activity the same way that he dismissed the fig tree and the Temple.

star; they fall out of the sky and the darkness swallows them up. They had no genuine interest in the spiritual well-being of Jude's readers.[73]

These false teachers are as dangerous as reefs, as selfish as greedy shepherds, as deceptive as rainless clouds, as dead as barren trees, and as polluted as the foaming sea.[74] They might seem smooth and impressive with their charismatic ways, but Jude's readers should not be deceived. They will be judged in the end: blown away, uprooted, and thrown into darkness.

Overpromising

One way that prosperity teachers disappoint their listeners is by giving them false promises. They teach us that as "the King's kids" in the Kingdom of God, Christians are now entitled to lives of material prosperity and perfect health in this fallen world. They declare that suffering, pain, and poverty are not the portion of a true believer because Jesus died to purchase good things for us. They teach that, because God desires prosperity for every one of his children, for a Christian to be in poverty or sick is to lack faith and to be outside God's intended will.

> No human being has ever lived as sinless, and as perfect a life as Christ did, and yet no human being has suffered as much as he did.

But the Bible does not promise us a trouble-free life right now. No human being has ever lived as sinless, and as perfect a life as Christ did, and yet no human being has suffered as much as he did. On the eve of going to the cross, Jesus told his disciples, "In this world you will have trouble. But take heart! I have overcome the world" (John 16:33). The original Greek word that is translated as "trouble" in this verse means stress, pressure, sorrow, and all the unavoidable psychological and emotional sufferings we experience in our lives.

We suffer because of the Fall. The ground has been cursed and life has become difficult. Work is frustrating, sickness is a reality, natural disasters strike. Our relationship with creation has been broken. We suffer because of the sins of other people, who hurt, abuse,

The New Testament says little about God's interest in our material success, but it speaks often of God's interest in our holiness.

demean, neglect, lie to, or take advantage of us. Our relationship with each other has been broken. We suffer because of our own sins and mistakes. We act selfishly, form addictions, ignore God's wise counsel, or believe lies of self-hatred. Our relationship with God has been broken. As Christians, we also suffer because of persecution. The evil one and his forces want us to give up on Christ, and one of his strategies is attacking, discouraging, and deceiving believers.

The New Testament explains that we should expect suffering as Christians. Following Jesus in this fallen world will always entail one form of suffering or the other (Philippians 1:29; 2 Timothy 3:12). Spiritually, we battle temptations, doubts, and the uncertainties of living by faith in God. Physically, we face financial, emotional, and physical challenges, as well as the burdens of Christian responsibilities for a family or a church community.[75] The New Testament says little about God's interest in our material success, but it speaks often of God's interest in our holiness, our maturity in Christ, and our growth into the fullness of his image.[76]

In the face of suffering, Hebrews 12:1-13 encourages us to fix our eyes on Jesus Christ, who began our faith and completes it. God allowed Jesus to suffer, even though he was innocent and righteous. He was still in control and used that suffering to save us and sanctify us (Hebrews 10:10,14; 13:12). We, too, cannot suffer anything unless God allows it. His sovereignty enables us to trust that he is in control. Through the Holy Spirit he can use our suffering to make us holy and set apart for his use (1 Thessalonians 4:3; 5:23). Christ suffered much more for our salvation than God will ever expect us to suffer for him. This should encourage us when we suffer.

Hebrews 12 says that in the same way that fathers discipline their children, our heavenly Father disciplines us. Though it is very painful, this is evidence that our Father cares for us and is making us into the spiritually mature children he wants us to be. God's sanctifying work in his children is like parental training. Children are trained through difficult situations that demand self-denial and discipline, sustained pressures that require endurance during the process, or skills that demand years of practice to develop. If, on the other hand, things are made easy for children, they remain spoiled, and they lack mature character. The Lord's spiritual training, sometimes difficult and unnerving, does not allow that to happen in the lives of his children.

> Christ suffered much more for our salvation than God will ever expect us to suffer for him. This should encourage us when we suffer.

When we submit to what God is doing in our lives, our "feeble arms and weak knees" are strengthened. When a person breaks a limb, the physician needs to set the broken bone. This painful experience might seem brutal. But the patient who trusts his or her physician knows that the pain experienced is the necessary first step back to health. Trials prove and test the genuineness of our faith (1 Peter 1:6-7; James 1:2-4; etc.). In the same way, our attitude to the Lord's painful work of sanctification should be the words of Hebrews 12:12, "Strengthen your feeble arms and weak knees!"[77]

In all these painful trials in this world, however, we can cling to the truths of the gospel. We know that, on the cross, Christ overcame the world and Satan. He defeated death itself. At our rebirth, his life is imparted into us by the Holy Spirit, giving us his strength and victory to endure and overcome our suffering. In addition to this, because of God's sovereignty, we are assured that nothing will ever be able to separate us from the love of God that is in Christ Jesus our Lord (Romans 8:38-39).

This perspective may not seem fair right now. Take a look at Psalm 73:4-5,

> They have no struggles;
>> their bodies are healthy and strong.
> They are free from common human burdens;
>> they are not plagued by human ills.

Is this describing believers' reality today? Read verse 12,

> This is what the *wicked* are like –
>> always free of care, they go on amassing wealth
>> (emphasis added).

The psalmist was confused when he saw "the prosperity of the wicked" in contrast to his own life of innocence and affliction. But it finally made sense when he saw the bigger picture. He realized the final destiny of the wicked was judgement, and then he understood God's ultimate justice. In contrast, he realized that he had God's presence in the present moment and in his glorious future:

Nothing will ever "be able to separate us from the love of God that is in Christ Jesus our Lord" (Romans 8:38-39).

> Yet I am always with you;
>> you hold me by my right hand.
> You guide me with your counsel,
>> and afterwards you will take me into glory
>> (Psalm 73:23-24).

The Bible promises us a glorious future. In eternity, suffering will be the portion of unbelievers. For believers, Christ "will wipe every tear from their eyes. There will be no more death or mourning or crying or pain, for the old order of things has passed away" (Revelation 21:4). But this won't happen until the end of time when Christ returns to this world to consummate the Kingdom of God (Revelation 11:15). Then God will once again dwell with his people in his Kingdom here on earth, just as he originally intended.

> Christians live prayerfully in the tension between the aspects of God's Kingdom we see *already* and *not yet*.

So how do we understand our position as "the King's kids" in the Kingdom of God? There is a part of the Kingdom of God that is here *already,* present with us spiritually. Christ came preaching that the Kingdom of God is here. Christians who have placed their faith in Christ have now been born again and entered this spiritual Kingdom of God (John 3:3 and Revelation 1:5-6).

But the full reality is *not yet* here. God's Kingdom will only be fully manifested in physical and material power and glory with the return of Christ to finally restore God's original Kingdom purposes for his creation.

So, for now, Christians live prayerfully in the tension between the aspects of God's Kingdom we see *already* and in anticipation of our eventual eternal destiny, which is *not yet* our current experience until Christ's return. For instance, John wrote, "*now* we are children of God, and what we will be has *not yet* been made known. But we know that when Christ appears, we shall be like him, for we shall see him as he is" (1 John 3:2). Paul talks about how we are saved and reconciled with God, but we are also "being saved" (1 Corinthians 1:18; see also Romans 5:9-10). We wait eagerly for the day when we will appear in glory with Christ when he appears in his second coming (Colossians 3:4).

Right now, we experience suffering, but one day we will experience glory (Romans 8:17). So, we can see, the prosperity doctrine is right about *what* blessings Christians can hope for, but wrong about *when* we can expect them. We can compare their teaching, too, to clouds without rain or autumn trees without fruit. They build their listeners' expectations of blessing, but at the time when you expect them to produce these blessings, the blessings don't materialize.

Pastor Daniel's Story

Shepherds should care for their sheep, not exploit them for financial gain. Pastors should care for the poor and the weak, not ignore them because they cannot profit from them. Preachers should give people the real hope of the gospel, not false promises of an easy life or motivational talks that will leave them struggling in their own strength. The church's witness is damaged when we don't live up to these standards. But when we live out these gospel-focused values, we bring real hope and transformation to people's lives.

I want to end this chapter with a story of a godly shepherd who preaches the gospel and offers hope to suffering people. Pastor Daniel was born to a Muslim family in Uganda. At the age of six, Daniel lost his father. His mother struggled to eke out a living for her six small children. Then civil war forced them to flee from the capital city, Kampala, to find refuge in the bush. Together with other hapless families, young Daniel's family scrounged to survive for two long years.

Eventually, as the civil war came to an end, the Red Cross helped Daniel's family return to a bare existence back in the capital city. Then one of Daniel's younger sisters got seriously sick. No medication seemed to help. One of their neighbours recommended that the child be taken to a local evangelical church to be prayed for. Daniel's Muslim mother initially refused. As her daughter's condition grew worse, however, she relented and took the girl to the church. The pastor laid hands on the sick child and prayed a simple prayer. Lo and behold, Daniel's sister was completely and miraculously healed!

Daniel's mother converted to Christianity. Her Muslim relatives disowned her. The church, however, helped her to start a small business selling fried snacks in the neighbourhood. The church enabled Daniel to receive support from World Vision, who paid for Daniel's primary and secondary education. After high school, Daniel joined the evangelical church as an active member. He began to grow in understanding the gospel and to love the Lord. He eventually became a youth leader in this church.

In 2006, Daniel was part of a mission trip to neighbouring Kenya. In a sprawling slum in Nairobi called Mukuru, Daniel encountered greater poverty than he had known in Uganda. Daniel also witnessed deep spiritual poverty, perpetrated by a host of prosperity churches who promised the struggling slum dwellers financial breakthroughs if they tithed enough. Daniel felt a burden to minister to these people.

In answer to prayer, his church eventually partnered with an American church that offered to sponsor Daniel. Daniel arrived in Nairobi with one US dollar in his pocket, but with tons of faith in his heart. Through a series of God-ordained connections, Daniel started a Bible study in the small home of a hairdresser in the slum.

In 2011, a fire swept through the slum. It destroyed 5,000 makeshift homes and displaced countless families. The Red Cross provided blankets and arranged temporary housing for the displaced families in a neighbouring working-class school that had closed for the holidays. Eventually Daniel and his growing Bible study group were also allowed to meet on Sundays in the school.

Today, 10 years later, the small Bible study fellowship has grown into a vibrant church. I regularly visit this church, and I can testify that they preach and teach the gospel. All giving is used to help struggling men and women in the community. Many widows have been assisted to start small businesses. The church acquired 20 sewing machines. Young women who were at risk of ending up as prostitutes or sexually abused single mothers have become skilled income-generating seamstresses. The church has provided inexpensive water filters that now supply clean drinking water to 15,000 households in the community.

Many girls in these slums are married off at the age of 13 or 14 or they are sexually abused by the time they reach 18 years of age. But the hairdresser's daughter, Grace, recently graduated from college with a Diploma in Information Technology. The church paid for Grace's primary, secondary, and college education, and sponsored over 30 other children as well.

Out of hopelessness and despair, many unemployed young men trapped in these urban slums end up as drug addicts and small-time criminals. In partnership with an American Bible-based ministry to drug addicts, the church reaches out to these addicts in the slum, helps them to get off drugs, evangelizes them, trains them with marketable skills, and guides them to become responsible examples to other desperate young men.

Whenever I preach in this church, I have a palpable sense of God's love. There is a genuine hunger for the Word of God. I always come away uplifted and encouraged by the spirit of love and hope I sense there. This is the difference our communities can experience if we have shepherds who care for the sheep, who preach the contents of the gospel, and who practically demonstrate the implications of the gospel in their lives and ministries.

Questions for Reflection and Discussion

1. Have you ever worried, like I did, that obeying God will mean you don't have enough money? How have you seen God faithfully provide for you?

2. How do you think God feels about people who are unsaved, poor, vulnerable, or sick? What does your church do to care for them, or what could you do?

3. What are some ways you see God's Kingdom here already? What are some ways you see it is not here yet?

4. What inspiring stories can you share of pastors who care for the people in their congregations?

Hope

CHAPTER 8
TRUE HOPE IN THE GOSPEL

*. . . They are clouds without rain, blown along
by the wind; autumn trees, without fruit
and uprooted – twice dead . . . (Jude 12).*

After the Overcomer's Hour service that Wednesday morning, I went upstairs to the senior pastor's office. Framed photos of the church's pastors decorated the walls. From behind a large desk, he told me that at least 1,000 people showed up for that mid-week service, and 2,500-3,000 came to the three Sunday services.

"The Wednesday crowd is a different lot from the Sunday attendants," he said. "They have different needs." I thought to myself, *Do they have such different needs that they don't need to hear the gospel preached? The deepest need of every human is the gospel that saves us.*

The pastor escorted me from his office to the air-conditioned board room, where five young pastors from citywide branches of the church were waiting for us, including the pastor who had led the Overcomer's Hour service. We sat in leather upholstered seats around a shiny boardroom table, with a large conference TV screen on the wall. The young pastors wore expensive-looking attire, watches, and footwear. They carried smart phones and iPads. I gave them my research questionnaire to fill out, and, as they did so, they asked intelligent questions.

They seemed to know all about the gospel. How was it, I wondered to myself, that they preached instead about planting seeds, as I had just witnessed? What explained their focus on material affluence that kept church members like the young woman who sat next to me, with their hard-earned cash, flowing in?

Later that day, I met with another pastor of another one of the large new churches in the country. The founder of this church was well-known for his miracle-offering programmes on national TV. Once again, the church compound was impressively developed, with a large parking lot, buildings that housed a primary school and offices, and a very large church hall, perhaps one of the most notable in Accra. This pastor too held a postgraduate degree from a recognized theological institution. His review of my doctoral research questionnaire was thoughtful and helpful.

I asked this pastor about the emphasis on the prosperity doctrine and miracles in his church. He replied that the theology that asserts that Jesus will bring prosperity is not unique to Africa but is common all over the world today. In America, he said, the teaching is spread through large and influential Christian TV networks.

The popularity of this teaching, he said, was because lives are indeed changed by it. Men in their church had become more responsible husbands and fathers who had now left alcohol and crime behind them. His church helped to rehabilitate street children, prostitutes, and drug addicts. They do not only teach prosperity, he said, they also teach business skills to young people out of school who could not find employment in the formal sector of the stagnant Ghana economy. Church members are encouraged to patronize each other's businesses and to network with one another. I was encouraged to hear about the church's social ministry.

Prosperity teaching, he said, inspired and motivated many people in the urban centres who would otherwise be without hope in the country's struggling economy. Jesus Christ did not just preach salvation; he also healed the sick and gave hope to the poor.

I agreed that Jesus's ministry was broad, although I replied that faithful preaching of the content and implications of the gospel would give true hope to the poor. This is why, he added, the church had cell groups where serious Bible study took place for their church members.

During my research I decided to ask some pastors why they did not preach the content and implications of the gospel in their churches. In almost every case, they said, "Oh, but we preach the gospel! After preaching the gospel, however, should we not then preach about how our church members can improve their lives?"

> The gospel is the solution to every problem Christians face in work, in relationships, or in interactions with non-Christians.

Their well-meaning response betrayed a commonly held misunderstanding about the gospel and its implications for every area of our lives. People think the gospel only concerns what a person needs to be saved, and then to progress in the Christian life people need to be taught more advanced biblical principles.

But the gospel is not only about how people get saved; it is about how their worldview is transformed. The gospel is the solution to every problem Christians face in work, in relationships, or in interactions with non-Christians.[78]

The church must preach the gospel, above all else, because this is what Christ himself modelled.

As we discussed in the previous chapter, Jude says the false teachers are like clouds that promise life-giving rain and trees in autumn that promise fruit – only to disappoint. People expect these teachers to offer life-giving teaching and spiritual nourishment, but the false teachers offer them fluff instead. Many people come to church expecting life-giving truth and spiritual food, but they find only preaching about prosperity, preaching on how to live moral lives, or a motivational speech. Let's look at the reasons why it is so desperately important for us to preach the gospel in our churches.

Why We Must Preach the Gospel

CHRIST MODELLED GOSPEL PREACHING

The church must preach the gospel, above all else, because this is what Christ himself modelled with single-minded devotion to his followers. When a group of people tried to keep him from leaving their town because they wanted more of his healing miracles, Christ emphatically said, "I must proclaim the good news of the kingdom of God to the other towns also, because that is why I was sent" (Luke 4:42-44). And he kept on preaching the good news of the gospel of the Kingdom in the synagogues of Judea.

CHRIST COMMANDED HIS DISCIPLES
TO PREACH THE GOSPEL

The church must preach the gospel because this was Christ's command to his disciples. He told them, "And this gospel of the kingdom will be preached in the whole world as a testimony to all nations, and then the end will come" (Matthew 24:14). After his resurrection and before his ascension, he said to them, "Go into all the world and preach the gospel to all creation" (Mark 16:15). By simply obeying and preaching the gospel, the apostles changed the world.

The church must preach the gospel because this was Christ's command to his disciples.

All the NT church's preaching was focused on the gospel. Paul declared, "Woe to me if I do not preach the gospel!" (1 Corinthians 9:16); "I am not ashamed of the gospel, because it is the power of God that brings salvation to everyone who believes: first to the Jew, then to the Gentile" (Romans 1:16). In Acts 20:24, as Paul reflected on the sufferings that could very well have been waiting for him in Jerusalem, he declared, "However, I consider my life worth nothing to me; my only aim is to finish the race and complete the task the Lord Jesus has given me – the task of testifying to the good news of God's grace." Paul was willing to die to preach the gospel!

Preaching anything else is dangerous. Paul declared that God will punish those who "do not obey the gospel of our Lord Jesus" (2 Thessalonians 1:8) and declared a curse on anyone, including angels, who preached anything other than the gospel (Galatians 1:8). The apostle James warned that those who teach in the churches "will be judged more strictly" by God (James 3:1). He was implying that those who teach anything other than the gospel would be held accountable by God for doing so. This means that the church's pulpit is reserved for the preaching of the gospel. It can be argued that any other *use* of the pulpit is therefore an *abuse* of the pulpit. This is because people without Christ are perishing, and we must preach the only thing that can save and transform them: the gospel.

Today, unfortunately, in many churches we find that preaching the gospel has been replaced with motivational talks about how people can fulfil their potential, talks that offer promises of material blessing conditional upon churchgoers giving enough tithes and offerings, and moralistic talks that call on churchgoers to be good and decent people.

> The church's pulpit is reserved for the preaching of the gospel. Any other *use* of the pulpit is therefore an *abuse* of the pulpit. People without Christ are perishing, and we must preach the only thing that can save and transform them: the gospel.

These motivational talks may stir emotions and spur listeners to short-lived action, but as we have discussed, our own efforts are unable to save us. So, the results of motivational talks are rarely lasting. Have you ever tried to change your life after getting good advice from a preacher? Too often our efforts fail, we fall back into old routines, and we despair. So, what do we do when another moralistic sermon begins? Our own consciences and proverbial cultural wisdom already teach us the moral standards the sermon offers.

We are all too familiar with the sense of guilt that comes from being told we are doing something wrong or that we are failing to live up to Christian ideals. So, we shut off to avoid the hopelessness that unavoidably follows the guilt.[79] Soon, church becomes nothing more than a social club where we go to meet people and engage in activities, rather than a place that promotes and encourages spiritual nourishment and growth.

These kinds of sermons just beat the will of churchgoers, trying to move them to live virtuously in their own strength and leaving them in quiet despair. Such replacements of the gospel only address the symptoms of our sinful behaviour, but the real gospel points us to the root cause. The gospel offers us a way out through faith in Christ. Church leaders must point people to how the gospel truly empowers their Christian living.

THE GOSPEL TEACHES CHRISTIANS
WHO THEY REALLY ARE

The third reason the church must preach the gospel is so that Christians understand that what the NT teaches is their real spiritual profile. We have explained how the heart of the gospel is that Christ suffered the death on the cross that our sins merited. He lived the God-pleasing life we weren't capable of living.[80] This is why, when we accept by faith his work on the cross for us, God credits us with the righteousness of Christ (2 Corinthians 5:21). The apostle John puts it in this remarkable way, "In this world we are like Jesus" (1 John 4:17).

Because of Christ's work on the cross and the Holy Spirit who lives in us, we are spiritually joined to Christ in the same way that Christ is spiritually joined to the Father – we are in him, and he is in us (John 14:20). Paul explained, "I have been crucified with Christ and I no longer live, but Christ lives in me. The life I now live in the body, I live by faith in the Son of God, who loved me and gave himself for me" (Galatians 2:20). Paul says Christians are so spiritually united to Christ that when he died, rose, and ascended to heaven, so did we (Romans 6:3).

This explains why Paul's letters describe Christians as being "in Christ" or "in the Lord" or "in him" more than 150 times. For example, Paul writes that when Jesus Christ was raised from the dead and was seated at the right hand of God, "God raised *us* up with Christ and seated *us with him* in the heavenly realms in Christ Jesus" (Ephesians 2:6, emphasis mine). Paul uses the past tense in this verse because he is not talking about something that will happen in the future, but rather, something that has already happened in the past when we placed our faith in Christ.

> Replacements of the gospel only address the symptoms of our sinful behaviour, but the real gospel points us to the root cause.

THE GOSPEL REMINDS US TO RELY ON
CHRIST'S STRENGTH AND THE HOLY SPIRIT

When we preach the gospel, Christians learn that they were never meant to live the Christian life in their own strength. We were meant to live only in the strength of Christ who lives in us by the Holy Spirit. The Holy Spirit works powerfully in God's people to bring moral change to their lives. Under the old covenant, in the Law, the people of God were told how to live in a manner pleasing to God, but they were not empowered to live that way (Hebrews 8:7-13). In the new covenant which Christ mediates (Luke 22:20), the Holy Spirit who lives in us gives us the life and power of Christ to enable us to live the way God wants us to live. This is the gospel.

> The Christian faith is not a religion of dos and don'ts, but rather, it is a relationship with God.

Church leaders must preach this gospel to help their people to know that the Christian faith is not a religion of dos and don'ts, but rather, it is a relationship with God the Father that is made possible by the work of God the Son on the cross and experienced in our lives by the empowerment of the in-dwelling Holy Spirit.

You have likely heard sermons that tell you to be an organized leader like Nehemiah, or to delegate responsibility like Moses, or to conquer the land like Joshua. You have heard sermons telling you to avoid sexual immorality, lying, stealing, or corruption. Perhaps you have preached some of these sermons yourself! You may be surprised to realize that these miss the mark of pointing us to Christ. Christ alone, by the in-dwelling Holy Spirit, empowers us to be all this. Christ reminded us of this gospel truth by saying, "I am the vine; you are the branches. If you remain in me and I in you, you will bear much fruit; apart from me you can do nothing" (John 15:5).

It is not our moral behaviour or even the quality of our faith that is the basis for our acceptance by God (Galatians 2:16). By God's grace, God gives us faith (Ephesians 2:8-10) that spiritually unites us to Christ. Christ's righteousness and his sinless record become legally ours. As a result of this saving faith, the Holy Spirit transforms our hearts to want to obey God out of gratitude and love, and the Holy Spirit gives us the power to do so (James 2:14-19).

When we replace the preaching of the gospel with dos and don'ts, we point people to the Law, away from Christ.[81] Paul says the Law was our schoolmaster to bring us to Christ so that we might be justified by faith (Galatians 3:24). In other words, the Law shows us our need for the gospel, so that we embrace God's salvation by faith. The Law then becomes the way we are guided to "grow into the likeness of Christ who has saved us."[82]

> As a result of this saving faith, the Holy Spirit transforms our hearts to want to obey God out of gratitude and love, and the Holy Spirit gives us the power to do so

Paul and the other apostles, who had all been raised as strict Law-keeping Jews, realized that the Christ event had fundamentally changed the basis of our relationship with God. Paul writes:

> We who are Jews by birth . . . know that a person is not justified by the works of the law, but by faith in Jesus Christ. So we, too, have put our faith in Christ Jesus that we may be justified by faith in Christ and not by the works of the law, because by the works of the law no one will be justified (Galatians 2:14-16).

Often after a new believer says "the sinner's prayer", they are presented with a raft of things they need to do, or not to do, to be accepted by God. This is the religious legalism that Christ, through the gospel, died and rose again to free us from (Galatians 5:1).

THE GOSPEL IS THE WHOLE POINT OF THE BIBLE

A final reason we must preach the gospel is the Bible itself. It is not just a book of laws and morality tales; it tells us how to experience God's salvation and blessing. The Bible tells one life-changing story. It is the story of God the Father's plan to save, redeem, and transform our lives through his final work on the cross of his Son Christ Jesus. It's the story of how the Holy Spirit within us empowers us to live in a manner that pleases God.[83] This is the glorious, amazing, gospel story of the Bible. Christ is the living Word of God (John 1:1), the point of the entire Bible story.

The Bible tells one life-changing story.

All Scripture invariably directs us to Christ and his salvation. Every OT prophet, priest, and king was pointing to Christ, the ultimate Prophet, Priest, and King. Every theme in the Bible finds its fulfilment in his life, death, resurrection, and ascension. Preachers must therefore point to Christ by showing that any given biblical passage is either a direct prophecy about him, or shows why he is necessary for us, or speaks about something that reminds us of him, or speaks about something that could not be accomplished without him, or shows us an individual or group of people like him.[84] Focusing on the Christ of the gospel is essential to understand and effectively preach any biblical text.

A good example of this is the story of the life of Joseph (Genesis 37–50), which follows a pattern of death and resurrection. Like Christ, Joseph is humiliated, rejected by his brothers and stripped of his glory-robe, becomes a slave of no reputation, and is presumed dead. Then he is exalted at the king's right hand, provides for the needs of his world, is discovered to be very much alive, and brings reconciliation to his family. Like Joseph, Christ suffered evil that resulted in the salvation of many (Genesis 50:20, Matthew 20:28; Acts 2:23, Romans 6:3-11). All effective preaching that handles the biblical text faithfully to preach the gospel must therefore inevitably preach Christ from all of Scripture.[85]

Expository Preaching

Over my many years of preaching, I have found that the most effective way of preaching the gospel is through expository sermons. Expository sermons start with a single passage of Scripture that contains one unit of thought, perhaps a section, a chapter, or a story. The preacher seeks to understand the original author's flow of thought by considering the genre, structure, and literary elements of the given biblical text.[86] The central idea of the sermon comes from the central idea of that Bible passage, and the main points of the sermon come from the original author's emphases. The preacher builds supporting points around the central idea of the passage. The applications the original author intended for his original audience guide the contemporary preacher's applications of the truths from the passage.

Some people take a different approach, called topical preaching, where the preacher begins with a topic such as "Finances" or "Marriage" and looks for multiple passages that could inform a Christian approach to this topic. Some people are drawn to topical preaching because it feels more practical. However, it is very easy for these sermons to become moral guidance instead of staying focused on the gospel. Focusing on a single passage keeps the preacher focused on the text instead of manipulating the text to say what he or she wants.[87]

It is still possible, for instance, to preach an expository sermon that preaches the gospel and its implications for our daily lives in our marriages. In Ephesians 5, the apostle Paul addresses spouses, especially husbands, many of whom had evidently come into the church with their non-Christian attitudes about marriage. In seeking to get the husbands to love, cherish, and honour their wives, Paul does not preach a moralistic sermon to them. Instead, he explains to them that as Christians, we are the bride of Christ.

To these husbands, Paul presents Christ as the ultimate husband who demonstrated sacrificial love for us on the cross not because we were sinless and lovely, but rather, to makes us lovely and acceptable to God by saving us from our sins. Christ was faithful to us at infinite cost to himself. Paul helps these husbands, and us, to see that we have all the affirmation we need in Christ to be loving and faithful to our spouses, no matter how difficult we may find it to "love" them.[88]

> Our churches and leaders should seek and support sound, evangelical, and contextual theological training to equip preachers with all they need to shepherd God's people faithfully.

One reason why preachers don't preach expository sermons is the time they take to prepare. To prepare an expository sermon, the preacher needs to understand the biblical text, create a clear outline of the text, identifying its main theme, and using appropriate illustrations and practical examples applicable to his congregation. No doubt, this requires many hours of hard and focused work of prayerful reflection on the text. Sadly, many preachers in our churches today simply do not give this kind of careful preparatory attention to their sermons.

Some preachers have not been theologically trained in balanced contextual understanding, interpretation, preaching, and application of the gospel. Paul counselled his protégé, Timothy, "Do your best to present yourself to God as one approved, a worker who does not need to be ashamed and who correctly handles the word of truth" (2 Timothy 2:15). Our churches and leaders should seek and support sound, evangelical, and contextual theological training to equip preachers with all they need to shepherd God's people faithfully.

Back to the Basics

I sat in the well-appointed boardroom of one of the churches I was visiting during my doctoral research. This boardroom was in an impressively large and well-constructed church building. This church was in one of the relatively new growing townships a few kilometres out of the city of Accra. Two decades ago, this township was just one of the many satellite towns that had sprung up on the far outskirts of the city. Today it had a significant population and, although many of its streets were still unpaved, large and impressive residential and commercial buildings were to be seen everywhere. This large and attractive church building reflected the upwardly mobile nature of this new township.

I was meeting with the senior pastor of this church. I had hit it off immediately with him. This senior pastor was a thoughtful and well-educated person with a doctoral degree from a prestigious theological institution. He had received me warmly and had granted me access to two other pastors of his church who had then filled out my doctoral research questionnaire.

I expressed to this church leader my concerns about the gospel-departing theology and the practices I had observed in the growing new churches in Ghana. "We have missed it," he said sadly. "We have missed the basics and turned the church into a bit of a marketplace."

I was surprised to hear him say this because he held one of the highest positions of national leadership in one of the largest, fastest-growing churches in Ghana in the last 20 years. I asked him what he felt could be done about this trend.

"We need to go back to the basics," he said. "We need to return to the simplicity of the gospel." Because of his high position in this church, his words gave me hope.

Questions for Reflection and Discussion

1. How is the gospel connected to any efforts we can make to improve our lives materially?

2. Which was your favourite reason for why we should preach the gospel?

3. Have you heard an expository sermon or preached one yourself? What did you notice about it?

God's Protection

CHAPTER 9

THEY DO NOT HAVE THE SPIRIT

*But, dear friends, remember what the apostles of our Lord
Jesus Christ foretold. They said to you, 'In the last times there
will be scoffers who will follow their own ungodly desires.'
These are the people who divide you, who follow mere natural
instincts and do not have the Spirit (Jude 17-19).*

During my doctoral research, I heard about the deliverance services
of a certain church. The founding pastor was considered to have
a special deliverance anointing. I wanted to witness this for myself.

The church met in a large hall that was formerly a cinema. The
hall was packed. After an hour or more of singing and dancing, the
pastor arrived on the stage. The congregation welcomed him with
much enthusiastic applause.

"Praise the Lord!" he shouted, waving a white handkerchief above
his head.

"Hallelujah!" the congregation yelled back.

"We are going to set people free today! All those witches and demons in your family are going to flee today!" he declared.

"Hallelujah!" the congregation yelled, some of them waving their handkerchiefs too.

The pastor then came down from the stage and began to walk through the aisles. He would point to someone and declare a prophecy over them. Two women fell in a swoon when the pastor pointed to each of them. He said to one man, "Is it true that your uncle fell sick last week?" The person said yes. He put his hand on the man's forehead and yelled, "I cast out these witches from your family, in the name of Jesus!" Back on the stage, the pastor spoke loudly in an unintelligible language and waved his hands over the congregation. In response, many people fell backwards. This happened three times.

The pastor descended the stage again and began to walk through the congregation. He would select a person and pray over them.

He told a woman, "It's a good thing you came here today. Let me tell you what I see over your life. I see that you would have been involved in a ghastly road accident that would have killed you." The poor woman was shaking in terror. "Now that you have come here, we are going to cast out that accident. It will not be your portion."

He said to another man, "Have you been passed over for a promotion in your place of work? The reason is that there are malevolent relatives who are using witchcraft against you. They are stopping your material success." He grabbed hold of the man's arms and shook him as he prayed, "I bind these forces in the name of Jesus. I declare victory over you."

After more energetic singing and dancing, it was time for the offering. The people who had been supposedly delivered were especially expected to contribute. Members of the congregation danced forward to place their offerings in the offering box located at the front of the church, just beneath the stage.

The pastor then asked those who were trusting God for healing to raise their hands. Then he asked those looking for visas to seek greener pastures abroad to lift up their passports. Those who wanted to pay their rent arrears or to own their own homes should raise door keys. Those who wanted jobs were asked to raise their cell phones. This went on until virtually everyone in the hall had raised either their hands or an object that symbolized what they were trusting God for. Then he prayed a loud, lengthy prayer, accompanied by drumming.

Jude's Exhortation

Jude had said in verse 3 that his purpose for writing the epistle was to urge his readers to contend for the gospel. In verses 17-23, he finally arrives at the heart of his appeal. Here, he switches from talking about the false teachers and now addresses his readers head-on: "But you, yourselves, remember!" Like a parent using her or his child's name when giving the child a command, Jude mentions "you" twice as if to say, "Pay attention! I'm talking to you!"

In the face of false teaching, Jude's readers must "remember what the apostles of our Lord Jesus Christ foretold." Jude turns the ears of his readers from the voice of the OT prophets he has so far been quoting to the more contemporary voice of Christ's apostles that still commanded their attention. Some of his readers, it appears, personally heard the apostles warn that false teachers would almost certainly appear to haunt the church with heresies and divisions.

> These false teachers will certainly not escape God's severe and inevitable judgement.

Jude then gives the fundamental reason God will surely judge the false teachers and their followers. He makes a bold assertion: the false teachers "do not have the Spirit." Paul said, "If anyone does not have the Spirit of Christ, they do not belong to Christ" (Romans 8:9). In other words, the false teachers were not even true Christians, despite all their claims to the contrary.

This sobering truth about the false teachers' real spiritual profile explains their immorality, their unbelief, and their idolatry. Jude called the false teachers "scoffers". They ridiculed, ignored, and scoffed at sound doctrine; they refused to heed God's instructions about righteous living. They lacked the Holy Spirit who is, after all, the Spirit of holiness. Without his presence in a person's life, they cannot desire or demonstrate holiness in their lives.

Jesus tells a parable about how he plants wheat, the people of his Kingdom, but Satan plants weeds, his people, in the same field (Matthew 13:24-28, 36-43). Satan plants false teachers in the church, using their ability and charisma to deceive God's people. He may even give them success and help them attain leadership positions where they can undermine the work of Christ and his gospel. Eventually, their ungodly character, their lack of integrity, and their love for money betray these teachers for what they really are.[89] Even if it doesn't happen until the end of the age, these false teachers will certainly not escape God's severe and inevitable judgement.

Among false teachers today, I believe there are people who have never known Christ and who Satan has planted. I also believe there are some people who were once nominal Christians and have fallen away. Others began their ministry in sincerity and truth, even though they might not have been well-trained in the content and implications of the gospel. But as they progressed in their ministries, spiritual immaturity, pride, and immoral desires led them into error. Satan could have taken advantage of this, even though they still thought of themselves as ministers of righteousness (2 Corinthians 11:15).[90]

Preachers can demonstrate impressive charisma and giftedness. They can perform miracles, heal, and deliver. This is a blessing when it is used to promote the gospel, but dangerous when it is delinked from the gospel and harnessed instead to the false prosperity doctrine.

"But they seem so spiritual!" Jude's readers might have protested.

Even today, don't some of our preachers seem very spiritual? They exhibit supernatural signs like miracles, deliverance, and speaking in tongues. Could it be possible that some of them do not have the Spirit? Could it be that, like Jannes and Jambres (2 Timothy 3:8), they use the powers of evil spirits?

Prophecies and Gifts of the Holy Spirit

Since the Holy Spirit indwells us to empower our holy living and to guide us to know the will of God (John 16:12-15), people often pretend they have the Spirit by claiming to know the hidden will of God. Jude condemned the false teachers for offering up their dreams as visions to justify their ungodly teaching and behaviour (Jude 8).

Some church leaders describe themselves as prophets, offering to reveal God's hidden will for their church members' lives and occupations. As part of my doctoral study of church teaching and practices in Ghana, I visited two of the leading "prophets" in the country. One asked to see my right palm. He read my palm and offered me a generic ATR-influenced prophecy about evil forces in my family who were fighting my material success. I discovered that this was very similar to what he told most people who consulted him.

I visited the other so-called prophet with a business friend. He predicted that my friend and I would together soon build a very successful export business. This has not happened, and indeed will not happen, because the business friend has since passed away.

Deuteronomy 18:22 alerts God's people that if what a prophet proclaims in the name of the Lord does not take place or come true, that is a clear indication that the Lord has not spoken. That prophet has spoken presumptuously.

In the years since I consulted them, these two "prophets" have grown very wealthy. Some people have accused them of operating with familiar spirits. While I cannot be sure of that, I know that any power they had did not come from the Spirit of truth, and that whatever wealth they had acquired was not a sign of God's approval.

Some people may say that certain people have the Spirit because those people demonstrate the gifts of the Spirit. They could be apostles with impressive charisma and leadership gifts or pastors with powerful preaching skills. They might receive words of knowledge or discern between spirits. They might perform healings and miracles, speak in tongues, interpret tongues, or engage in dramatic deliverance rituals.

Many churches are known for their deliverance sessions. Church members go through spiritual rituals that may involve them screaming, crying, wailing, galloping, jumping, slithering, falling asleep, collapsing and sometimes, even appearing to be dead.[91]

However, when Christ cast out demons in the Gospels, he simply commanded the demons to leave. When the all-powerful sovereign God saved my staff and me from the demonically inspired attacks against our lives and our business, we did not have to resort to any rituals. Our faith in Christ and his redemptive presence in our lives was all we required to experience his powerful protection.

Some years ago, as I was undertaking a three-day fast, a troubled young man came to see me at home. I had been trying to assist him spiritually and financially. After I had laid hands on him and quietly prayed for him, he suddenly fell back in the chair, unable to stand. Then, he suddenly began to tremble. When he tried to get up from the chair, he fell back into the chair. Then, suddenly, he fell on the floor and began to slither like a snake, yelling to be left alone.

I realized immediately that this was a manifestation of demonic oppression. I called my wife, and together, we prayed over him. A few minutes later he lay still on the floor. We prayed over him some more. Then he weakly got up from the floor, with tears streaming down his face. He said he now felt much better. Clearly, our prayers over him had been used by the Lord to deliver him from demonic oppression.

> By overemphasizing the fearful power of demons and overcomplicating the deliverance process, leaders keep people dependent on them for protection and security.

After this unexpected power encounter, it occurred to me that genuine deliverance should be undertaken in more private settings, such as happened to this young man in our home. Genuine ministries of deliverance should not be undertaken to bolster the minister's pride. They should be acts of love relying on the delivering power of the risen Christ to set men and women free from demonic oppression, continuing the ministry Christ began on earth which included much deliverance.

For this reason, I suspect that in many of our churches that purport to have a deliverance ministry, these public dramatic rituals and emotional reactions are unnecessary for the person being delivered. However, they are very useful to make an entertaining show for the audience, whether the congregation or viewers on television. The more dramatic the scene, the more afraid the viewers become, and the more powerful the person who performs these feats seems. By overemphasizing the fearful power of demons and overcomplicating the deliverance process, leaders keep people dependent on them for protection and security.

Regardless, even performing miracles and driving out demons are not failproof signs that someone is a true Christian.[92] Like the false teachers Jude describes, Jesus says some miracle workers were never his true followers. Jesus warns his disciples:

"Not everyone who says to me, 'Lord, Lord,' will enter the kingdom of heaven, but only the one who does the will of my Father who is in heaven. Many will say to me on that day, 'Lord, Lord, did we not prophesy in your name and in your name drive out demons and in your name perform many miracles?' Then I will tell them plainly, 'I never knew you. Away from me, you evildoers!'" (Matthew 7:21-23).

Because miracles can be counterfeit, it can be very difficult to tell when someone performs miracles in Jesus's name whether they are truly operating on his authority.

I believe Christ says some miracle workers were never true followers of Jesus Christ because miracles and signs can be counterfeited by the evil one. For instance, in Exodus 7–11, Moses confronted Pharaoh and his magicians with the power of God. Aaron threw down his staff and it became a snake. But Pharaoh's diviners each did the same. When Aaron struck the water of the Nile and it turned to blood, Pharaoh's diviners did the same. When Aaron made frogs come up and cover the land, Pharaoh's diviners did the same.

However, the power of Pharaoh's diviners had a limit. Aaron's staff-snake swallowed up the other staffs that were turned into snakes. The diviners were not able to make gnats appear. They could not compete with the plagues of flies, livestock, boils, hail, darkness, and death of the firstborn; in each of these cases, the Lord ensured the plagues touched only the Egyptians, not the Israelites in Goshen. At some point, the diviners could not even appear before Pharaoh because they were covered in boils. God is almighty and sovereign over every power and principality.

> Church leaders offer themselves as modern-day diviners with special powers to deliver church members from evil forces, find promotion or material success, and protect them against enemies.

Not Trusting in God

The diviners of Egypt were not as powerful as God's appointed leaders. But the main difference between them was that Moses and Aaron urged Pharaoh to believe in the true God, and the Egyptian diviners hardened his heart, urging him to trust in their false gods instead. Are our pastors more like the diviners of Egypt or are they operating in the true power of the Lord? Ghanaian Pentecostal Bible scholar Joseph Quayesi-Amakye encourages us to consider the similarities between diviners in ATR and leaders in our churches today.[93] I believe that knowingly, or unknowingly, many of our pastors today encourage us to have faith, not in God, but in them and in their methods.

When people go to a diviner in ATR, they are looking for deliverance from evil spirits, poverty, and ill-health. The recommendation to solve their problem will usually involve objects such as talismans and potions, performing rituals, special phrases as incantations, and sometimes sacrifices or libations involving blood. Of course, one must pay the diviner for these services.

Because many African churchgoers still confront their problems through the prism of ATR thinking, they still seek the services of a specialist, a diviner, who they believe can explain to them what is happening in the supernatural realm of spirit beings. Church leaders offer themselves as modern-day diviners with special powers to deliver church members from evil forces, find promotion or material success, and protect them against enemies.

Congregants are often instructed to use objects one might call talismans to get their healing or deliverance or breakthrough. This might involve using the Bible or a hymnbook as if there is magical power in the object itself.[94] People may be instructed to pour "anointing" oil on objects such as congregants' bathrooms, toilets, garbage cans, floors and entrances to homes, handkerchiefs, door keys and car keys, cell phones, passports, and business documents. Church leaders may call church members to the front and blow air into their faces, or sprinkle "anointed" water or oil on their bodies or faces, telling them that this will make them experience the power and presence of the Holy Spirit.

The church leaders may perform deliverance rituals to eliminate the threats of satanic powers and give church congregants access to divine favour and assistance. Often, church members are told to perform a certain action to receive their blessing, like unlocking the door with keys as I saw in the service that Wednesday morning, or dancing, or raising their hands, or attending the kind of deliverance service described at the beginning of this chapter.

Incantations and prophetic declarations are also common, often using a formula that invokes the blood of Jesus or the name of Jesus as if it is a spell. For instance, people may repeat "The blood of Jesus covers me" as a formula. Prayers use the language of warfare to "demolish the strongholds" of spiritual enemies. Prayers are often long, sweaty, and muscular, almost as if to give people visible proof of the effort of fighting. They often involve declarations as, "You spirit of poverty, sickness, disease, bad marriage, shame, embarrassment, disappointment, today as I raise my hands to heaven, I command you in the name of the Lord Jesus Christ to leave me now! I command the fire of heaven to consume you right now!" These declarations are understood to be displays of spiritual empowerment.

Churchgoers are encouraged to trust in talisman-like objects, phrases used in prayer, and rituals. They learn to go to the "man of God" or the prophet with their problems and trust that person to intercede for them in the spiritual realm. But Christ is our only mediator, and we have direct access to God as a result of his sacrifice on the cross (1 Timothy 2:5; Hebrews 4:16).

Deuteronomy warns about false prophets whose predictions do not come true, but it also teaches that even if someone's prophecy or sign comes true and they urge us to follow other gods, we must not follow that prophet (Deuteronomy 13:1-4). God made the prophet's prediction come true to test whether we love God with our whole hearts. These teachers use wonders and signs to point people away from trust in God towards false gods.

> Many churchgoers in Africa today have merely traded one set of diviners for another, but this time, in the church.

Since these practices are often tied to deliverance from witchcraft, demons, and Satan, they often lead to an unhealthy preoccupation with the powers of evil, rather than with God himself. [95] To encourage people to be delivered, people often proclaim all the ways evil could have power over one's life. Demons are asked to speak through possessed people, giving them the microphone in a church service. Churchgoers learn to attribute all their sinful habits, trials, and difficulties to witchcraft. When it mirrors ATR practices most closely, it can even lead to accusations that individuals in the church are harming others through witchcraft, which creates hostility, fear, and hatred.[96]

Quayesi-Amakye concluded, from his interactions with many pastors and prophets, that some of the so-called prophets went to the extent of acquiring occult powers to engage in these practices and to exercise unrestrained influence over their church members.[97] Several times during my own doctoral research, I came across this assertion from different quarters.

Sadly, this suggests that many churchgoers in Africa today have merely traded one set of diviners for another, but this time, in the church. This is especially evident in the fact that people pay for these services through their tithes and offerings, purchasing anointed objects, and so forth. These church leaders have therefore been frequently accused of being motivated by a vested interest in maintaining churchgoers' fear of evil forces because it helps them to attract and keep members. We should reject all attempts by prosperity preachers to offer us protection through special prophecies and prayers for a fee; they are only extorting money from us. Only the risen, exalted, and ascended Lord on high can offer us true protection (Luke 10:19).

> We should be wary of church leaders who loudly claim the work of the Holy Spirit in their ministries, but in whose lives we see no sign of the character of Christ.

The Fruit of the Spirit

How, then, are we to discern that someone is a true prophet? Jesus said, "A good tree cannot bear bad fruit, and a bad tree cannot bear good fruit . . . Thus, by their fruit you will recognise them" (Matthew 7:18, 20). Jude had already mentioned that the false teachers were like autumn trees without fruit. This is how he knew they lacked the Holy Spirit. They lacked the fruit of the Holy Spirit in their lives, such as self-control. They were led, not by God, but by their sexual instincts and ungodly desires.

In fact, Jude had denounced the false teachers' godless character and conduct for the majority of his letter through verse 16. He mentioned their ungodly actions and their evil desires. Their mouths were also ungodly, with defiant words, grumbling, fault-finding, boasting, and flattery. In verses 14 and 15, Jude used the word *ungodly* four times in various forms. He was making a point: God will severely judge the false teachers and those who follow them when Christ returns to this world at his Second Coming with thousands upon thousands of his holy angels.

As Charles Price, the British church leader and scholar, puts it, "The devil can counterfeit the gifts of the Spirit . . . but he cannot counterfeit the fruit of the Spirit for it is an expression of the very character of God, and [the devil] hates that!"[98] We should be wary of church leaders who loudly claim the work of the Holy Spirit in their ministries, but in whose lives we see no sign of the character of Christ.

The Holy Spirit reproduces in us the very character of Christ. When a person says they are an American, they mean that they come from America. When I say I am a Ghanaian, I mean that I come from Ghana. In this same way, when we say we are Christ-*ians*, we mean that our inner spiritual life comes from Christ. This life of Christ is imparted into us by the Holy Spirit: "We know that we live in him and he in us: he has given us of his Spirit" (1 John 4:13).

The life of Christ that the Holy Spirit imparts into us at our new birth is our spiritual DNA that henceforth shapes and determines our spiritual growth and transformation into the character of Christ. In our own willpower and strength, we cannot duplicate the character of Christ in our lives. Only Christ can live the Christ life. This is what Christ meant in John 15:5 when he told his disciples that, "I am the vine; you are the branches. If you remain in me and I in you, you will bear much fruit; apart from me you can do nothing."

In Galatians 5:22-23, the apostle Paul referred to the character of Christ that the Holy Spirit produces in us as the fruit of the Holy Spirit: "love, joy, peace, forbearance, kindness, goodness, faithfulness, gentleness, and self-control." These are the character qualities that made Christ attractive and appealing to everyone who met him. "Fruit" in this verse has the idea of "result" in the same way we say, "the fruit of your hard work is your success." Christ's character reproduced in us is the fruit produced when we yield more and more to the leading and direction of the Holy Spirit in our lives.

> Fruit is always for the benefit others, not itself. The Holy Spirit produces his fruit in our lives, which gives people a taste of Christ's character.

Fruit is always for the benefit others, not itself. The Holy Spirit produces his fruit in our lives, which gives people a taste of Christ's character. People around us are hungry for love, joy, peace, and patience. As the Spirit bears this fruit in us and we offer it to others, we provide them nourishment from Christ's character.[99] The world around us then sees in us the character of Christ that made him so attractive to the people who met him and to whom he ministered during his earthly ministry.

The fruit of the Spirit, like physical fruit, takes time to grow and mature in our lives.

When we come to God through Christ, we now belong to God's family. The Father wants to see us behaving like one of his children, especially like our elder brother Christ, as we now display the fruit of the Spirit in our lives. Therefore, becoming a child of God is always marked by a change in a person's character. "In this world we are like Jesus" (1 John 4:17); the Lord says of his disciples, "you are in me, and I am in you" (John 14:20). Paul declared, "I have been crucified with Christ and I no longer live, but Christ lives in me" (Galatians 2:20). The gospel teaches that the definite result of our salvation is that Christ might come and live his life within us by the Holy Spirit.

Sometimes the change upon conversion can be dramatic.

- The Philippian jailer bathed the wounds of the bruised and battered evangelists he had imprisoned (Acts 16:31-34).
- The Ethiopian eunuch went on his way rejoicing after his baptism (Acts 8:39).
- Zacchaeus repaid those he had cheated, fourfold (Luke 19:8).
- Nicodemus eventually committed himself publicly to the cause of the gospel (John 7:50-52; 19:38-42).
- Saul who had zealously persecuted the church became Paul, the self-sacrificing missionary of the church.

Normally, however, unlike the gifts of the Holy Spirit that we receive from God in a one-time experience, the fruit of the Spirit, like physical fruit, takes time to grow and mature in our lives. We allow this to happen in our lives as we deliberately choose, in the power of the Holy Spirit, to respond with Christ's:

- love to people who we would not ordinarily be able to love,
- joy to depressing circumstances,
- peace to difficulties and anxious situations,
- patience to all that calls for impatience,
- kindness to those who are mean to us,
- goodness to bad people and bad behaviour,
- faithfulness and gentleness to deceitful and rough people, or
- self-control to temptations or situations that make us lose our cool and make us want to seek revenge.

Both the gifts and the fruit of the Holy Spirit were evident in the life of a respected Christian leader I knew. This leader, now deceased, was the secretary-general of a major evangelical institution and an elder in one of the largest churches in Kenya. On a couple of occasions, I went to discuss pressing personal matters with him. Both times, he said to me, "Okay, let's bring this to the Lord in prayer." Just before he prayed, he paused with his eyes closed and clearly received a word of knowledge about the situations we were going to pray about. I know these were words of knowledge received from the Lord because there was no way he could have known about these things, but I recognized them immediately as relating to my situation. This was a simple yet profound demonstration of the gifts of the Holy Spirit. In addition, he demonstrated the fruit of the Holy Spirit by being very humble, generous, loving, and self-effacing. In my season of difficulty and affliction, he offered me financial assistance even though he himself, at that time, had been diagnosed with the cancer that eventually ended his life.

While it may be discouraging and disconcerting for us to realize that some of our leaders do not have the Spirit, I want to end with the encouragement Jude offers in the first part of these verses: "But, dear friends, remember what the apostles of our Lord Jesus Christ foretold. They said to you, 'In the last times there will be scoffers who will follow their own ungodly desires.'" While the church was experiencing upheaval as a result of scoffers and false teachers, Jude reminded them that the apostles had told them to expect this in these last times. We, too, live in the last times, the time between Christ's first and second coming. We can draw encouragement from the fact that our struggles with false teaching and division are predictable. God forewarned the apostles. God is still sovereign and in control of this situation.

> Our struggles with false teaching and division are predictable. God is still sovereign and in control of this situation.

Questions for Reflection and Discussion

1. Think of someone known in your context as a prophet. Using the guidance from this chapter, can you discern whether he or she is a true or false prophet?

2. Why can the evil one counterfeit the gifts of the Spirit but not the fruit of the Spirit?

3. What do you think it would look like to practise deliverance in the simpler, less publicly dramatic way that Jesus delivered people? What changes might your church need to make to do this?

Power of Love

CHAPTER 10
PROTECTING OURSELVES

But you, dear friends, by building yourselves up in your most holy faith and praying in the Holy Spirit, keep yourselves in God's love as you wait for the mercy of our Lord Jesus Christ to bring you to eternal life (Jude 20-21).

After building up his argument against the false teachers from verses 1 to 19, in the rest of the letter, Jude finally does what he had set out to do from the beginning: he urges his readers to contend for the faith. Once again, he calls his readers to attention: "But you, dear friends." In verses 20 to 23, he gives the readers two lists, each containing three exhortations on how his readers can practically contend for the faith. What is the first thing they absolutely must do in the face of all this false teaching? He gives them a command. The imperative in these two verses is "keep yourselves in God's love".

Keeping Ourselves in God's Love

If you have been reading this book and wondering what to do in your context when you are confronted with false teaching, Jude's response here is instructive. Knowing his readers were confronted with false teaching, Jude's first command was not to go to the media to denounce the teachers publicly. He didn't tell them to start a rival radio or television station or to go on social media. He didn't even tell them to prioritize a seminary education. He told them to keep themselves in God's love.

Keeping ourselves in God's love is the best protection against false teaching. Just before he was crucified, Jesus told his disciples to anticipate persecution. But first, he gave him this command: "As the Father has loved me, so have I loved you. Now remain in my love. If you keep my commands, you will remain in my love, just as I have kept my Father's commands and remain in his love" (John 15:9-10).

In 1 John, John writes to a church dealing with false teaching. But he spends a great portion of his letter reminding the readers of God's love for them. Because they are children of God, they should demonstrate that by loving others.

This makes sense, because doubting God's love is often the root issue when people fall away. The first false teacher, the serpent, tempted Eve to believe that God was withholding something good from her. Our first parents doubted God's love for them, even though this was in abundant display all around them in the Garden. This is why, in Hosea 6:7, God declared that Adam refused his love.

The Israelites in the wilderness, when faced with hunger, began to doubt God's character, thinking that God had brought them out into the wilderness to die of hunger or be killed by their enemies. Their deception began with the feeling that maybe God couldn't be trusted, and that God wasn't going to provide everything they required to meet their needs. They doubted if God really loved them.

The prosperity doctrine tells us, "You need to give the church money. Then, God will bless you." But if we are confident in God's love for us, we can easily respond, "I don't need to do anything to make God show me he loves me. He has already given me his only Son!" (John 3:16; Romans 5:8).

In Luke 15, Christ compared our heavenly Father to the father of the prodigal son. The son asked his father for his inheritance early, implying that he wished the father was dead already. He lived a careless lifestyle and squandered his wealth. But when the father saw the son coming back home, he did not need any convincing to throw the son a huge party to welcome him home.

The prosperity doctrine suggests that we need to buy God's love. It suggests that the signs that God loves us are the jobs, spouses, cars, breakthroughs, and healings that prosperity preachers falsely promise us. It is like a child who makes sure that she gets good grades in school so that her parents give her gifts. Perhaps her parents never seem to have time for her. Maybe they are always travelling for business, they are swallowed up by addiction, or they have left her to be raised by her grandmother or the house-help. When the girl gets that gift for her good grades, she takes it to school and tells all her classmates, "See! My parents love me!"

But deep down, she feels that if she doesn't get good grades, they may not even feed and clothe her. She doesn't have any confidence in their love. She is showing off her gifts at school because she is still desperate for affirmation, if not from her parents, at least from having nicer things than her peers. She needs someone to agree with her that her parents love her, because she is really unsure.

> False teachers and the evil one can counterfeit truth with their teaching or power with their miracles. However, they lack love, because God is love.

Contrast that with a child who is secure in his parents' love. He doesn't worry about what he will eat or whether his parents will buy him clothes. His parents show him their love every day. Their smiles, encouraging words, shared activities, and touch remind him that he is their son. They might give him gifts for good performance, but they will also show him love when he is hurting, sad, or angry.

Love is simply the most powerful transformative and liberating emotion known to human beings.

Our deep inner awareness of God's love is therefore a powerful response to false teaching. False teachers and the evil one can counterfeit truth with their teaching or power with their miracles. However, they lack love, because God is love.

Love transforms us. To use a simple example, when I was in secondary school, my boys' boarding school had extracurricular activities such as school debates and drama events with various girl schools across the country. The school leadership didn't want us to grow up completely ignorant of girls and their ways. At the age of 16, as shy as I was, I mustered up the courage to talk to my crush from one of those girl schools.

Those were the ancient days when there were no mobile phones and no Internet. So, this girl and I promised to write to each other. Sure enough, the following week, she wrote telling me that she liked me. Wow, she likes me, she likes me! I was ecstatic. I must have read that letter a million times! I put it under my pillow and took it out every day. My school friends would sometimes ask, "Why are you smiling like that?" I hadn't realized I was smiling. This first experience of falling in love, even if it was just a fleeting adolescent infatuation, made me feel affirmed and valued.

Love, in its various forms, is simply the most powerful transformative and liberating emotion known to human beings. Experiments have shown that babies shrivel and die without the tangible experience of being loved by their mothers. Every year, hundreds of songs, plays, films, and books are produced that celebrate love. Without love, we feel unwanted and abandoned. If human love makes us feel so affirmed and valued, imagine how much more God's divine, unconditional love could change our lives! If only we would allow it to become very real to us deep in our hearts.

In Romans 5:5, the apostle Paul writes that when we become Christians, God's love is poured out into our hearts through the Holy Spirit. The indwelling Holy Spirit, in other words, gives us both the ability to experience God's love within ourselves, and the ability to demonstrate this love to others. This explains why one of the apostle Paul's pressing items of prayer for the Ephesian Christians was, "May your roots go down deep into the soil of God's marvelous love; and may you be able to feel and understand, as all God's children should, how long, how wide, how deep, and how high his love really is; and to experience this love for yourselves" (Ephesians 3:17-19, TLB). Through the gospel, we can come to experience deep in our hearts God's unconditional love, the greatest love of all. What Christ did for us on the cross displays God's love for us, foremost and for ever (John 3:16). When we respond in faith to the gospel, the Holy Spirit makes God's love real to us. When we personalize the gospel in our lives, we consistently see God's love as he provides for our needs, protects us, and gives us his peace in our peaceless world.

> What Christ did for us on the cross displays God's love for us, foremost and for ever (John 3:16).

Building Yourselves Up in the Most Holy Faith

Then Jude describes what his readers should do to keep themselves in God's love: by building each other up, by praying in the Holy Spirit, and by waiting for the mercy of our Lord. He has described what the false teachers are doing, now he says "*but you*, dear friends" must do the opposite. The false teachers tear down our faith, *but you*, build yourselves up in the faith. The false teachers do not have the Spirit, *but you* pray in the Holy Spirit, because you, unlike the false teachers, have the Holy Spirit. The false teachers can only expect judgement upon Christ's return, *but you* wait for the Lord's mercy.

Building yourselves up in your most holy faith echoes back to verse 3, when Jude said he "felt compelled to write and urge you to contend for the faith that was once for all entrusted to God's holy people". As we discussed already, the faith here refers to the gospel. Jude's readers are to hold firmly to the gospel truths handed down to them by the apostles Jude has just mentioned in verse 17.

Jude's counsel echoes what Paul said to Timothy, who faced false teaching in Ephesus. Paul emphasized Bible study, telling Timothy to be a worker "who correctly handles the word of truth" (2 Timothy 2:15). Paul reminded him in 2 Timothy 3:12-17:

> In fact, everyone who wants to live a godly life in Christ Jesus will be persecuted, while evildoers and impostors will go from bad to worse, deceiving and being deceived. But as for you, continue in what you have learned and have become convinced of, because you know those from whom you learned it, and how from infancy you have known the Holy Scriptures, which are able to make you wise for salvation through faith in Christ Jesus. All Scripture is God-breathed and is useful for teaching, rebuking, correcting and training in righteousness, so that the servant of God may be thoroughly equipped for every good work.

Both Timothy and Jude's readers needed to continue in the true faith they had received, and the Scriptures were their essential resource to build themselves up. The truths of the gospel would equip them for good works, just as the false teachers' lies had equipped them for ungodliness.

In Jude's instruction, the word "yourselves" is plural. A communal, corporate, and committed study of the Word of God will bind these believers together. This contrasts with the false teachers' divisive refusal to engage in such an active and sincere study of God's Word in the assembly (Jude 19).

Several years ago, I began to feel burdened about my Bible teaching ministry in our church because, although I was teaching and preaching the gospel regularly there, I wasn't sure I was reaching my fellow church members with the gospel in a transformative way.

I felt the Lord was calling me to start an interactive discipleship programme particularly for the men in the church. I prayed about this for about a year. The Lord brought to my attention a particular Bible study programme being used effectively around the world. With the blessing of the senior clergy, I asked the men in the church if they were interested in trying it.

They responded enthusiastically. Although these were busy professional men and business executives, they made it a point to regularly attend each Tuesday night. We bonded as we mutually learned from God's Word, shared our prayer concerns and prayed together, and shared refreshments. It provided real encouragement and spiritual growth for us all. A couple of them who were not Christians became Christians and grew in their faith.

Two years later, the Lord began to impress on me that they needed to lead their own individual Bible study groups. We prayed about this together. I organized a training session for them, paired them in twos, and they established small Bible study groups in their respective neighbourhoods. To this day, these various Bible study groups are still growing. We still meet as a group, but now, only once a month.

The men have taken up various leadership roles in the church. It is a real joy to see their continuing spiritual growth, their love for the Lord, and their growing interest in serving the Lord in the church.

At the time of this writing, one of these Christian men is one of five Court of Appeals justices who have recently protected the interests of the general public by preventing senior politicians from changing Kenya's constitution in favour of parochial political interests.

Through Bible study, praying together, and community, we build up ourselves and one another. We strengthen our faith and gain insights into the implications of the gospel for our daily living that enable us to grow spiritually.

Praying in the Holy Spirit

Another way to keep ourselves in God's love is by praying in the Holy Spirit. Jude could be referring to various forms of Spirit-inspired prayer, one of which is praying in tongues.[100] Pentecostals traditionally understand praying in tongues as a God-given capacity that is valuable to heighten a Christian's mood of praise, penitence, and petition.[101] Jude may very well have been present at Pentecost when the Holy Spirit enabled believers to speak in other languages, so he may very well have had this in mind. Elsewhere in the NT, we see that Paul agreed that praying in tongues is a way by which Christians edify themselves (1 Corinthians 14:4), but he also strongly addressed abuses of tongues in the Corinthians' public worship.

Jude teaches that engaging in Spirit-inspired prayer is essential for the church, but I think that today, as in the church in Corinth, we have gotten off-track from the original intent of the Spirit-inspired prayer that Jude had in mind.

The city centre branch of one of the churches I researched for my doctoral studies received several warnings from the City Council. Many nearby businesses complained about the noise and distraction caused by their loud praying in the middle of the working day, which was broadcast through amplified loudspeakers. Like most capitals, Accra is full of noise: honking traffic, street vendors advertising their wares, public transport vehicles whose speakers blare music, news, or preaching.[102] For people to complain about noise in this city is saying something.

That church relocated to a large church building in a residential area of the city and kept up their loud Friday all-night prayer sessions. The church blasted loud guttural noises and chanted unintelligible words, believing this to be Spirit-anointed praying in tongues. Even the nightclubs stop at a certain hour, but the church was heard all night. Their neighbours repeatedly asked the church to reduce the noise, but nothing happened. Finally, the community lodged a court case against the church.

When I found out about this, I asked one of the church leaders if the loud praying could not be reduced or curtailed to attract their neighbours to join the church rather than attracting their ire and displeasure. This church leader responded to my question by saying that the Bible calls upon Christians to engage in effectual fervent prayer. But wasn't the second most important commandment to love our neighbours?

The church leader's reference to effectual fervent prayer came from James 5:16-18. James cited the example of Elijah, who prayed that there would be no rain in Israel, and sure enough, there was no rain.

> When James concluded from this story that "The effectual fervent prayer of a righteous man availeth much" (KJV), what he meant is simply that praying in faith according to the will of God is powerful and effective.

Again, he prayed that there would be rain, and there was rain.

Elijah had boldly declared to the idolatrous King Ahab that there would be no rain (1 Kings 17:1) because he knew the will of

God. In Deuteronomy 28:15, 23-24, God had decreed that one of the consequences the Israelites would suffer from idolatry would be a lack of rain in their land. Ahab and his wife had introduced widespread idolatry throughout Israel. Because Elijah was praying according to the revealed will of God, God honoured his Word revealed in Deuteronomy 28 and withheld rain from Israel. When James concluded from this story that "The effectual fervent prayer of a righteous man availeth much" (KJV), what he meant is simply that praying in faith according to the will of God is powerful and effective.

> When we measure prayer in terms of its loudness, its length or its eloquence, we show that we have misunderstood our relationship with God.

Unfortunately, this church's prayer resembled what Jesus warned against when he said, "And when you pray, do not keep on babbling like pagans, for they think they will be heard because of their many words" (Matthew 6:7). In contrast, Jesus introduced the simple Lord's Prayer for his disciples. We see an example of the contrast between pagan and Christian prayer in Elijah's story. When Elijah and the servants of Baal met on Mount Carmel, the pagan prophets called on Baal from morning until noon and danced around their altar.

> At noon Elijah began to taunt them. "Shout louder!" he said. "Surely he is a god! Perhaps he is deep in thought, or busy, or travelling. Maybe he is sleeping and must be awakened." So they shouted louder and slashed themselves with swords and spears, as was their custom, until their blood flowed. Midday passed, and they continued their frantic prophesying until the time for the evening sacrifice. But there was no response, no one answered, no one paid attention (1 Kings 18:27-29).

Elijah's taunting revealed that the pagans believed God would hear them according to the volume, duration, and desperation of their prayer. It is a common ATR belief that saying "the right things in the right tone of voice accompanied by certain right words and actions [yields] right results."[103]

Witch doctors and fetish priests, like the pagan priests of Baal in 1 Kings 18, spend long hours engaged in loud incantations and rituals to appease dark spirits and solicit their aid on behalf of people in need. It is troubling to notice similarities within churches today, where people believe it is only when "anointed" church leaders pray for us that our prayers will be answered.

It is not that praying loud or lengthy prayers is wrong in itself, aside from its effect on our neighbours. But when we measure prayer in terms of its loudness, its length, or its eloquence, we show that we have misunderstood our relationship with God.

Jesus also taught his disciples that, in contrast with the hypocrites, they should not pray in public to be seen by others. They should go into their rooms, close their doors, and pray in secret (Matthew 6:5-8). In prayer we know that we are speaking to our Father, so we speak simply and directly. God is our loving Father who knows our needs and who is ready and able to help us. Having prayed as we are led to do by the Holy Spirit, we can have the confident expectation that, in whatever way our Father considers best for us, he will answer us.

> If prayer is twisting God's arm and forcing him to do our will by our fervency, it means God has become our servant, and we have become his master. Any prayer that receives a favourable answer from God first begins with him and his will.

We pray "your will be done" as Jesus did and align our prayers with what he has revealed to be his will, as Elijah did. If prayer is twisting God's arm and forcing him to do our will by our fervency, it means we have reversed the roles. God has become our servant, and we have become his master, so that he must do whatever we please.

Any prayer that receives a favourable answer from God first begins with him and his will. "This is the confidence we have in approaching God: that if we ask anything according to his will, he hears us. And if we know that he hears us – whatever we ask – we know that we have what we asked of him" (1 John 5:14-15). Romans 8:26-27 further assures us that, even when we do not know what we ought to pray for, the Holy Spirit intercedes for us in accordance with the will of God.

I recently had a dream that was more of a vision from the Lord. My sister Monica in Ghana had telephoned me to say, "Kwasi, Mama is gone." I was sad and alarmed. As the firstborn in my family, the death of my mother during a tough pandemic time seemed to me the worst kind of financial challenge possible. Every time my sister called, I panicked that she would tell me my mother had passed away.

My mother soon fell ill. Seven weeks after my dream-vision, my sister called me and said those exact words. I still felt sad and anxious about raising funds for a Ghanaian funeral. But through our good friends and family, the Lord adequately provided everything we needed to give my mother a good send-off, including safe travels to Ghana and back to Kenya.

> Praying in the Holy Spirit refers not only to praying in tongues, but also to praying in line with God's will, which the Holy Spirit reveals.

I now see that the Lord was trying to prepare me for my mother's departure and to reassure me that he would take care of it all. Our heavenly Father knows what we need even before we ask him (Matthew 6:8).

As we pray in accordance with the Holy Spirit's leading, we grow into spiritual maturity. It increases our faith in God, our awareness of his presence and love with us, and our tangible experience of his daily provision and protection for us.

This is why when Jude talks about "praying in the Holy Spirit", I believe he was not only referring to praying in tongues, but also to praying in line with God's will, which the Holy Spirit reveals to us.

For instance, one morning soon after the birth of my daughter, Yaa Henrika, I woke up early to pray. I received a disturbing vision of a child being wheeled on a hospital stretcher with the mother anxiously dabbing beads of sweat from the child's forehead. I prayed for the child and the mother in the vision.

When I finished, as I prepared to leave home to go to the office, my wife informed me that a few minutes earlier, a heavy glass-framed poster had fallen from the wall onto the pillow where baby Henrika normally slept. Without understanding why she had done so, my wife had moved the child a few minutes earlier from the bed and taken her to the living room. The poster would have smashed into the forehead of the baby. Goose bumps covered my body as I realized the meaning of the vision that I had received from the Lord.

> If the incarnate Christ developed intimacy with his Father and received guidance through prayer, how much truer must it be for Christians!

In the experience above, the Holy Spirit led me to pray for my loved ones in accordance with God's will. Being led by the Holy Spirit is a common experience of many Christians. Spirit-inspired prayer is a blessed gift of the Christian life, a discipline which Jude urged his readers to regularly engage in. When we make daily devotional prayer a regular part of our lives, we develop intimacy with the Father. We learn to hear his voice more clearly and receive his directions for our daily Christian lives.

Even Jesus spent time in prayer to hear the Father's will. In Mark 1:21-39, Jesus had spent a tiring day of ministry in Capernaum.

After he healed Peter's mother-in-law, crowds heard the news and brought all their sick and demon-possessed friends and relatives to camp at Peter's door. I like to imagine that Peter told the crowds, "Dear friends, the Master is tired. The food my mother-in-law has prepared for him is getting cold. Please take the rest of your sick relatives home. The Master is spending the night here in my house and I can assure you that he will still be here to attend to them in the morning."

> Habits of early morning prayer help us to avoid plunging head-long into the day without reference to the Lord.

I imagine Peter woke up to the commotion of the crowd gathering outside his front door, only to find the room where Jesus had slept the night before was empty. Peter was in shock. What would he say to his neighbours?

Mark 1:35 tells us that "Very early in the morning, while it was still dark, Jesus got up, left the house and went off to a solitary place, where he prayed." When Peter and his companions found the Lord praying alone on the outskirts of the town, they exclaimed: "Everyone is looking for you!" (1:36-37). Instead of returning to meet the needs of the crowd, Jesus replied, "Let us go somewhere else – to the nearby villages – so I can preach there also. That is why I have come."

Why did Jesus change his itinerary? He declared elsewhere, "The Son can do nothing by himself; he can do only what he sees his Father doing, because whatever the Father does the Son also does" (John 5:19). I believe the Father had made it clear to Christ that his work that day was to be elsewhere, not in Capernaum. Jesus took time to listen to and to obey the Father's directions rather than being led by Peter's promises to the crowd. If the incarnate Christ developed intimacy with his Father and received guidance through prayer, how much truer must it be for Christians!

Habits of early morning prayer help us to avoid plunging head-long into the day without reference to the Lord, as if our own strength and wisdom can successfully carry us through the day. Habits of prayer help us to discern the Lord's voice so we can pray in line with the Holy Spirit's will. Whether we pray in tongues or in our own languages, this is what Jude had in mind for his readers, in contrast to the gospel-distorting men who did not have the Holy Spirit. Praying in the Holy Spirit keeps us in God's love because we realize that he delights to reveal his will to us and needs no convincing to hear and answer our prayers.

> He delights to reveal his will to us and needs no convincing to hear and answer our prayers.

Waiting for the Lord Jesus Christ

Where there is life, there is hope. So goes the popular saying. While this is true, it is probably truer to say that, where there is hope, there is life. This is because human beings are hoping creatures.[104] Most of our activities are shaped by our hopes and our anticipations. We get married hoping to live happily ever after; no one anticipates divorce. We invest in a business hoping for business success; no one expects business failure and bankruptcy. We go to school hoping to acquire marketable skills that will launch us off into wonderful careers; no one anticipates unemployment. Parents bear children hoping to have brilliant, obedient, and loving children; no one anticipates rebellious and wayward teenagers. When we are sick, we hope to get well, and on and on goes the list.

Hope, in the NT, however, does not refer to mere expectation and desire, but rather to trust and assured confidence in that which is certain to happen.[105] In the NT hope is never a vague optimism about the future, but rather, a solid certainty about the future. This is why, in Titus 2:13, Paul called the Second Coming of Christ the blessed hope of the church.

When Jude exhorts his readers to "wait for the mercy of our Lord Jesus Christ to bring you to eternal life", he would have his readers think about what it will be like to stand before God and enjoy his presence for ever at the Second Coming of Christ. Jude was reminding his readers to expect Christ's conclusion of their salvation at his Second Coming. In contrast, at the Second Coming, the false teachers' unsaved condition, false teaching, and disobedience to Christ would only merit the Lord's severe judgement.

> In the NT hope is never a vague optimism about the future, but rather, a solid certainty about the future.

Many of our churches today rarely teach about the Second Coming of Christ. The focus is on church members pursuing a perfect life of health and wealth in the here and now in this fallen world. The prosperity doctrine encourages churchgoers to happily settle for the best this world can give them. It limits our hope in this world to making money and finding a measure of satisfaction in our material possessions. As we discussed in an earlier chapter, we do have hope for a trouble-free life, but only some aspects of God's Kingdom are *already* here. The complete fulfilment is *not yet* our reality.

Ghanaian Pentecostal scholar and educator Kingsley Larbi has argued that the traditional African understanding of salvation has to do with the enjoyment of long life, health, and wealth in the present. The focus of ATR activity is obtaining good harvests, children, health, and long life in this world. There is little vision for what happens after death or another future world; even those who were good people merely become ancestors whose primary purpose is to assist people still in this world. Larbi suggests that Africans easily accept the prosperity doctrine because of its similarity with the traditional African understanding of salvation as the key to abundant life and the enjoyment of wealth and health in the here and now.[106]

The situation is not much better in the church in the developed world. The "soft prosperity gospel" is equally seducing many churchgoers in America from the glorious hope of the real gospel of Christ. People believe that working hard for God guarantees that God will work hard for you, resulting in good kids, a nice house, a steady job, and plenty of money. People neglect Bible reading and prayer, and they wonder how God could allow them to suffer.[107]

When we focus on living the good life in the here and now, we lose interest in the Second Coming of Christ. We ignore God's deep abhorrence of our sin and believe we have a right to expect from God health, wealth, ease, excitement, and sexual gratification in this world. But our ultimate ease is only reserved for Christ's Second Coming, not for life in this world, which will never be perfect because of sin.

In contrast to this, Jude exhorts his readers to focus their hearts and minds on their Christian hope that, based on the gospel truth of God's grace and mercy for us displayed by Christ on the cross, one day we are going to live in God's presence for ever when Christ returns to this world the second time.

> When we focus on living the good life in the here and now, we lose interest in the Second Coming of Christ.

On the last pages of the Bible, the apostle John presents a glorious vision of Christ's Second Coming (Revelation 21:1-4). In whatever way one may choose to interpret the apostle's words in this passage, they at least point us to the fact that at Christ's Second Coming God will finally restore his eternal Kingdom here in this world, just as he intended it to be in the beginning, and our world will once again be a world without sin, suffering, and death. The words of Revelation 21:1-4 remind us of our gospel hope that Christians are a pilgrim people travelling through this world who, "are on our way home, and home will be glorious".[108] On this pilgrimage home, we can trust the Lord to answer us when our prayers echo these words from Proverbs 30:8-9:

> Keep falsehood and lies far from me;
>> give me neither poverty nor riches,
>> but give me only my daily bread.
> Otherwise, I may have too much and disown you
>> and say, "Who is the Lord?"
> Or I may become poor and steal,
>> and so dishonour the name of my God.

Pressing towards heaven does not keep us from improving our communities. We still heed Jude's exhortation in verses 20 and 21 of his epistle to live out the implications of the gospel in our daily lives. As with the example of Pastor Daniel's church, Christians have started literacy classes and clinics, helped alcoholics and drug addicts and prostitutes find new lives, listened to and counselled husbands and wives about how to resolve their conflicts, and taught parents how to better nurture their children.

Jude shows us that in the face of false teaching, our priority must be to allow God's unconditional love for us to shape our thinking and our behaviour, individually and as a church community. This love is ultimately displayed by Christ on the cross and announced to us in the gospel. Jude knew that without a deep inner experience of the reality of God and his love for us, life ultimately has no meaning at all. Knowing God loves us shields us from the allure of false teachers' promises to give us what only God can give us.

Several years ago, I fell very ill with hepatitis B. In just a year, I had lost my business, my money, and now, I had lost my health. My head-knowledge told me that God still loved me and that my suffering was not a result of sin in my life or that God had somehow abandoned me. But I was very beaten down by all the suffering that I was going through. I felt discouraged trying to reconcile what I knew in my head with what I was feeling.

One early morning as I prayed, the Lord used 1 Peter 4:13 to minister very powerfully to me: "But rejoice inasmuch as you participate in the sufferings of Christ, so that you may be overjoyed when his glory is revealed." From this verse, somehow, the Lord powerfully assured me that all suffering and pain will end for God's people with the Second Coming of Christ, when his full glory will be revealed to us.

Suddenly, my pain and suffering seemed to lose their sting. As I began to meditate on the Second Coming of Christ, my depression began to lift. I began to give thanks and praise to God. This mood of joyful expectation about the Second Coming of Christ stayed with me for several days. I later received physical healing and financial restoration. Looking back on it now, I notice that it began with the spiritual healing the Lord gave me in that epiphany.

Like Jude's readers, therefore, we will do well today to cultivate a daily awareness of God's love through the spiritual disciplines of engaging in Spirit-inspired prayer, studying God's Word together, and learning to live in eager anticipation of the Second Coming of Christ.

Questions for Reflection and Discussion

1. How do you feel when you consider the threats of false teaching around you?

2. Can you think of a time when you were tempted to doubt God's love for you? How does God's love protect us from being unfaithful to him?

3. How have you experienced praying in the Spirit, both in your personal life, and in the church?

4. What hope does it give you to meditate on the Second Coming of Christ? How could you bring this to mind more frequently?

CHAPTER 11

RESCUING OTHERS

Be merciful to those who doubt; save others by snatching them
from the fire; to others show mercy, mixed with fear – hating
even the clothing stained by corrupted flesh (Jude 22-23).

John Mensah grew up in a family of six children in a suburb of Accra. At the age of six, he was the first one in his family to begin to attend church, one of the older Pentecostal churches in the city.

At 17 years old, he chanced early one evening upon an open-air showing of *The Jesus Film*. At the scene with Christ on the cross, the speaker made an altar call: "Christ died painfully for you so that you would not have to face eternal death for your sins. Through his death and resurrection, you can have eternal life." The Holy Spirit powerfully convicted John. John was shy, so he didn't go forward, but he surrendered his life to Christ. The next day, John woke up with an inexplicably deep joy and excitement that he could only attribute to that prayer. He told everyone in his home and in his neighbourhood about Christ.

That same year John entered secondary school, where he joined the Scripture Union, an evangelical school-based discipleship ministry. The headmaster of the school was the SU patron. He took John under his wings and mentored him into leadership. During the school holidays, John played an active leadership role in the youth group in his church.

John went to university and joined the Ghana Fellowship of Evangelical Students (GHAFES). Lecturers at the university who loved the Lord mentored him, and he rose in the ranks of the GHAFES leadership. After graduation he got the opportunity to go to the UK for a brief course in Bible and expository preaching.

John took up the chaplaincy role at his former university, mentoring Christian students there. Eventually, John gained a scholarship which supported his master's degree in Pastoral Ministry in South Africa.

As John learned and was mentored through all these opportunities, he began to realize that he had grown up with legalistic theology that preached the need to obtain God's favour through moral efforts such as living a holy life, helping the poor, and converting others to Christ. He felt that the church he attended as a child had missed the freedom in Christ and the amazing grace of God that is at the heart of the gospel. He noticed that other churches, with their focus on material prosperity, also seemed to miss the true gospel.

Upon his return to Ghana, John became the associate pastor of an evangelical non-denominational church in a town a few kilometres from Accra. He realized legalistic preaching made churchgoers feel either fear of being punished by God for wrong behaviour or false pride from right behaviour as if it gave them some leverage over God. After studying in the US on another scholarship, John returned to Ghana to lead the West African branch of an international church planting ministry.

With support from financial partners, John has now planted a small gospel-focused church in Accra. The initial group of 12 adults and 7 children has grown to 40 adults and 37 children today. The church members are hungry for the Word of God. John is humbled and excited as he watches his church members grow.

Jude's final appeal to his readers indicates that the church he wrote to included church members with differing spiritual profiles. Those who were evidently mature in their faith were probably the people being given these instructions. Those who doubt might have been young in their faith, people who were genuinely concerned and inquiring, people who were convicted and seeking, or people in distress. Then, there could have been those, like the false teachers, who could be classified as either being unconverted, or who were at best, nominal and religiously self-satisfied churchgoers. In short, Jude was describing a congregation very much like many of our own very mixed congregations today. Let's examine how Jude guided his readers to respond to the threat of false teaching with these different groups in the church in mind.

Discipleship and Spiritual Formation

In verses 22 and 23, Jude now exhorts his readers to contend for the gospel by actively engaging in the mission of God. In verse 22, with the phrase, "be merciful to those who doubt", Jude spoke about people who may have had hesitations or doubts about the gospel because of the influence of the false teachers. These were likely to have been believers who were at risk of being swayed from the faith. Because these members are vulnerable, Jude instructed his readers to be merciful to them. People should accept and love these wavering members to encourage them. They should gather them in with forgiveness and a willingness to understand their vulnerability.

A response of harsh and legalistic rejection would only drive them into the arms of the false teachers.

If you know believers who are beginning to listen to misleading preachers or music, who are beginning to question the basics of the faith, or who are drawn to services or communities where false teaching is spreading, Jude's advice here applies to you. If we simply wring our hands in defeat and despair, we will have failed to contend for the gospel and allowed false teaching to continue to have its harmful way in our churches. Instead, seek the Lord's guidance and help. Show these believers that you are concerned about them. Look for ways to invite them into personalized and focused discipleship and spiritual formation. Offer them love and encouragement, even as you gently point out the difference between false teaching and the truth of the gospel.

Help these believers become disciples, a word that means *learners*. This word was used for an apprentice or an intern who attached himself to a teacher in order to learn a trade or a subject. Disciples undergo a form of practical training by watching and doing. This explains why, throughout the Gospels, Christ consistently explained that if we want to be his true disciples, we need to watch him so that we can do what he did and go in the same direction as he went.

Michael, who we met in a previous chapter, felt troubled and disillusioned by the immorality of some of his church leaders and their emphasis on finances. He fasted and prayed and sought guidance from the Lord. He began to study the Bible for himself.

A friend invited him to join a small Bible study group. As he grew in his understanding of the Word of God, he realized that the Scriptures that supported the practices that troubled him had often been misinterpreted. For instance, he realized that in the NT, Christ seldom talked about tithing. Many of the Scriptures the church leaders used to solicit funds from church members were OT passages taken out of context.

Michael saw that there was more emphasis placed on demons and fighting these demons than on the victory that Christians have in Christ. As Michael studied the Word of God for himself and as he developed intimacy with God through a growing prayer life, he told me that he experienced the joy of the Lord.

Michael eventually joined a small non-denominational church. In this church, Michael was happy to note that the emphasis on tithing and sowing seeds was absent. He made friends with older Christians in this church who answered questions he had about the Christian faith. The preaching in this church focused on Christ and the gospel. The church was involved in outreach to the community and they gave to those in need. He has become involved in the youth ministry in this church, teaching and mentoring many young people in the church. All this, Michael told me, had resulted in his steady and continued spiritual growth in Christ.

Evangelism

Next, Jude tells his readers: "save others by snatching them from the fire; to others show mercy, mixed with fear – hating even the clothing stained by corrupted flesh." His language comes from Zechariah 3:1-7,

> Then he showed me Joshua the high priest standing before the angel of the Lord, and Satan standing at his right side to accuse him. The Lord said to Satan, "The Lord rebuke you, Satan! The Lord, who has chosen Jerusalem, rebuke you! Is not this man *a burning stick snatched from the fire?*"

> Now Joshua was dressed in filthy clothes as he stood before the angel. The angel said to those who were standing before him, "Take off his *filthy clothes*."

Then he said to Joshua, "See, I have taken away your sin, and I will put fine garments on you."

Then I said, "Put a clean turban on his head." So they put a clean turban on his head and clothed him, while the angel of the Lord stood by.

The angel of the Lord gave this charge to Joshua: "This is what the Lord Almighty says: 'If you will walk in obedience to me and keep my requirements, then you will govern my house and have charge of my courts, and I will give you a place among these standing here'" (emphasis mine).

The fire Zechariah described was God's judgement in the Babylonian Exile. The high priest represented Israel. Their sin was represented in the filthy clothes that made them unfit to enter God's presence. While Satan wanted to accuse Israel for all their sins, the Lord still had a purpose for them. God would strip the priest of his position, as well as his sin, and restore him to his position with righteousness from God.[109] God was willing to give Israel a second chance if they would repent and obey him.

Similarly, Jude was saying that his readers were in genuine danger of the eternal fire he referred to when he described Sodom and Gomorrah in verse 7. The situation was dire and urgent. However, even those who had corrupted and contaminated their bodies with sin were not beyond the saving power of God.

> Genuine Spirit-inspired repentance completely reorients our hearts, our minds, and our wills towards God.

These words remind us of John the Baptist, who warned people they were in danger of the fires of hell. He said, "The axe has been laid to the root of the trees, and every tree that does not produce good fruit will be cut down and thrown into the fire"

(Matthew 3:10), reminding us of Jude's description of the false teachers as uprooted, fruitless trees. Jesus would soon be harvesting the wheat and "burning up the chaff with unquenchable fire" (3:12), so people needed to confess their sins, repent, and produce fruit in keeping with repentance.

"Repent, for the kingdom of heaven has come near." These were the first words both John the Baptist and Jesus Christ spoke when they each began their ministries (Matthew 3:1-2; 4:17) and concluded Peter's first sermon at Pentecost (Acts 2:38).

In the NT the word *repentance* means more than just feeling bad or remorseful about our actions or behaviour. It means turning and changing one's mind about God and oneself so that one changes one's ways too. Genuine Spirit-inspired repentance completely reorients our hearts, our minds, and our wills towards God, which is demonstrated in our behaviour.

If I say, "I am saved" or "I am born again" but show no change in my life with reference to God and to sin, that shows that I have not produced fruit in keeping with repentance. As in Zechariah, after we are saved, the Lord calls us to walk in obedience.

Repentance is a work of the Holy Spirit deep in our hearts to convince us that we are sinners facing the wrath of a holy God (John 16:8). The Holy Spirit's repentance works in our hearts like antiseptic on a wound. The antiseptic may sting, but it heals. Repentance creates turmoil within us as the Holy Spirit confronts us with our pride, our self-righteousness, our rebellion, and our disobedience to God. But this inner turmoil leads to the healing of our spiritual sickness of sin, as we

> If I say, "I am saved" or "I am born again" but show no change in my life with reference to God and to sin, that shows that I have not produced fruit in keeping with repentance.

humble ourselves before God, and we receive his forgiveness and his peace in our hearts.

In verse 23, Jude's phrase, "save others by snatching them out of the fire" guided his readers on how to respond to those in their midst who were flirting with the errors of the false teachers, thereby courting the fires of hell. These people were already beginning to accept the gospel-departing teaching of the false teachers and to adopt some of their ungodly behaviour. These church members needed the more mature and spiritually grounded members of the church to support them morally and spiritually, rather than harshly ostracizing and dismissing them from the assembly. Jude's counsel to snatch them out of the fire meant not rejecting even these misled members but calling them to repentance.

Jude appealed to his readers to engage in evangelism and bring the gospel to those in their midst who were not yet truly Christians. Evangelism is not only preaching the gospel to non-Christians outside the church to make them Christians through open-air meetings and door-to-door evangelism. As Jude's exhortations in these verses indicate, evangelism also involves faithfully bringing the gospel on Sundays to those in our churches who are church-*ians*, but not Christ-*ians*.

> Churchgoers have often been led to believe that Jesus will give them relief from poverty, sickness, and despair, and even make them materially rich, if they come forward and repeat a certain prayer. Tragically, this often does not include genuine Spirit-inspired inner conviction about sin.

This is a common problem in our numerically growing African churches today. While a recent survey recorded in Operation World shows that 64 per cent of Ghanaians were Christians, the Ghanaian Christian scholar Jones Darkwa Amanor says, "The extent to which the population was truly Christianized has, however, come under some scrutiny since the discovery, by the Ghana Evangelism Committee, that nominalism is the greatest problem of Christianity in Ghana."[110]

Part of the problem is that churchgoers have often been led to believe that Jesus will give them relief from poverty, sickness, and despair, and even make them materially rich, if they come forward and repeat a certain prayer. Tragically, this often does not include genuine Spirit-inspired inner conviction about sin.

As they repeat a prayer about following Jesus, they are often not told that Jesus expects his disciples to follow him to the cross. Being a disciple of Christ means picking up one's cross and even losing their life for the gospel (Luke 9:23-26). While God does bless us, following Jesus means paying the high price of self-sacrifice, just as Jesus sacrificed himself to be our redeemer.

A crucified Saviour, in other words, demands crucified followers and disciples. On the cross, Jesus lost his life so we could have eternal life. He was forsaken by the Father so that the Father might accept us. He exchanged his identity of righteousness with our identity as sinners so that we might have new identities as righteous, beloved children of God (2 Corinthians 5:21). For this reason, Christ says in Luke 9:23 that his disciples must "deny themselves", saying no to culturally conditioned responses to life. We must be willing to give up identities defined by our cultures and by what we do, so that we can truly have a new identity as the children of God. Can we call people to count the cost and follow Jesus, knowing that by losing their life they will really save it?

> A crucified Saviour, in other words, demands crucified followers and disciples.

A young lady called Mary was diagnosed with cancer. My wife, who was mentoring her, went to see Mary at the hospital. Mary told my wife that when she slept, she was haunted by nightmares in which dark and frightening monsters had come to take her away with them.

I knew that Mary had been raised in a large Pentecostal church. But I also knew from her lifestyle that she was not really walking with the Lord. Like the people Jude addressed, she was a church-ian, but not a Christian. When I heard about her nightmares, I sensed that the Lord was asking Mary to commit her life to him.

I went to the hospital and told Mary that the Lord was going to heal her either earth-ward to return to her family and her active athletic life, or heaven-ward to be with the Lord, if she had a relationship with the Lord. How the Lord would heal her was his decision, not the doctors' or anyone else's. I asked her if she was ready to meet the Lord if he chose to heal her heaven-ward.

She looked away from me and she mumbled something. So, I shared the gospel with Mary in a very, very simple way. She responded to the message by speaking directly to the Lord.

From that day on, Mary's nightmares ended. She had a new joy of the Lord in her eyes and in her smile. She shared the gospel with the other patients in her hospital ward and some of them came to know the Lord. When people went to see her, Mary shared the gospel with them. They went to encourage Mary but left being the ones encouraged! The hospital ward became Mary's church.

> As people are brought back into right relationship with God, they become the agents he uses to seek other lost people

After over a year in the hospital, Mary went to be with the Lord. Mary received both the spiritual healing of salvation, and eternal physical healing in the eternal presence of the Lord.

Evangelism is announcing the good news of the gospel to lost human beings so that they could be saved and brought into right relationship with God. God entrusts his continuing search for the lost to those he has already found. As people are brought back into right relationship with God, they become the agents he uses to seek other lost people, as we see in Mary's example.

Mercy Mixed with Fear

In verse 23, Jude's phrase, "to others show mercy mixed with fear – hating even the clothing stained by the flesh", appears to be directed at people who had been thoroughly involved with the false teachers, perhaps even the false teachers themselves. Like the high priest Joshua, their clothes were contaminated with sin; their carnal behaviour had corrupted their flesh.

By the expression "mixed with fear," Jude is implying that these people were to be approached cautiously. To be sure, they and their message were charismatic and enticing. There was a real danger they would contaminate the faithful members of the community with their gospel-departing teaching and ungodly behaviour. Then even more people would receive God's severe judgement.

So, anyone who sought to assist the false teachers needed to be aware that they themselves could experience temptation. While helping the fallen, they should not assume they were invulnerable to falling. They needed to hate every aspect of sin, even while believing that if God could redeem Israel from out of exile, he had the power to redeem even the most obstinate and deceived members of the community.

Resulting in Revival

Jude's appeal to his readers to engage in evangelism, discipleship, and spiritual formation was in obedience to the teaching of Christ himself. In what we call the Great Commission, Jesus Christ instructed his disciples to go into all the world and to make disciples through evangelism, and to teach them to observe all the things that Christ had commanded them through discipleship and spiritual formation (Matthew 28:18-20). Christopher Wright, the British church leader and Bible scholar, has famously written of the two-part Great Commission that, "It is not so much the case that God has a mission for his church in the world but that God has a church for his mission in the world."[111]

"It is not so much the case that God has a mission for his church in the world but that God has a church for his mission in the world."

The Scriptures show us what happens when we heed this call. At Pentecost in Jerusalem, the Holy Spirit's power came down. Peter, engaging in evangelism, called people to repent. Then the first NT church community engaged in discipleship and spiritual formation. They "devoted themselves to the apostles' teaching and to fellowship, to the breaking of bread and to prayer" (Acts 2:42). As a result, "the Lord added to their number daily those who were being saved" (Acts 2:47).

Repentance has transformed the African church before as well. In the 1920s, the missionary Dr Joe Church and his African co-workers of the Ruanda Mission, an arm of the Church Missionary Society, were burdened by how many people claimed to be Christians and yet mixed their faith with ATR practices and lacked spiritual fruit, so they unceasingly asked God for a visitation of the Holy Spirit.[112] For Joe Church, praying with Ugandan Simeon Nsibambi was a turning point in experiencing fresh strength from the Holy Spirit.

Soon afterwards, the Holy Spirit sent what came to be called the East African Revival. The Holy Spirit moved his slumbering and compromising church, setting believers on fire for the gospel and convicting unbelievers to repent and put their faith in Christ.[113] The gospel message that Christ had been crucified to save us was the centre of the revival.[114]

Conviction of sin drove people to repentance to the extent that the revival was characterized by public confessions of sin.[115] Revivalists spread across East Africa sharing their conversion testimonies and urging people to submit to Christ as Lord in all areas of life.[116] People met in revival fellowships to study God's Word, sing, share testimonies, and hold each other accountable. Evangelism and discipleship went hand-in-hand.

The revival resulted in countless healings, miracles, and much deliverance from witchcraft.[117] The East African church became known for prayer and unity; for 50 years the impact continued to energize Presbyterian, Anglican, and Methodist churches connected to the East African Revival.[118]

One legacy of the East African Revival was that every saved Christian was "expected to have a living testimony, a story of how Jesus had saved them, and from what."[119] We need this public confession and testimony in our churches, where emphasis on the prosperity doctrine has created an ignorance of the concept of sin.

The revival led to Christians focusing once again on the Second Coming of Christ. The revival "created a sense of urgency to live in right relationship with the Lord daily and to proclaim the gospel to those who had not yet come to Christ."[120] Is this not exactly what we need today?

> The revival led to Christians focusing once again on the Second Coming of Christ.

Throughout the Christian centuries, God has sent revivals to spiritually revitalize his church whenever she has been threatened by the kind of syncretism, nominalism, and departures from the gospel we find in our churches today.[121] The alternative to revival is always God's necessary and corrective judgement (Malachi 4:6).[122] The repentance described in the preceding section is possible if the Lord once again visits his church on the continent with a revival.

Revival, in other words, is the Christian church returning to the God-given and gospel-shaped norm we find in the NT.

Let's pray fervently for true repentance and a God-sent revival in our churches. This would genuinely spiritually transform our churches and our leaders, turn us away from teaching that has veered off from the gospel, and make us eager to unashamedly proclaim the gospel of Christ to the lost around us. True repentance and a God-sent revival will return our churches to the gospel and empower us to apply Jude's message to our work and ministry.

It is important to note that although Joe Church, Simeon Nsibambi, and their colleagues prayed for a spontaneous move of the Holy Spirit to bring revival, they were not passive. They also diligently taught the gospel and evangelized people for Christ. They heeded Jude's counsel to his readers to contend for the gospel. God responded by sending the East African Revival to revitalize his church.

If we are concerned about the false teaching and eager to see a revived African church, we need to heed Jude's exhortation here. We need to engage in gospel-focused and Christ-centred evangelism, discipleship, and spiritual formation, as we wait for the Lord to revitalize his spiritually languishing church.

Questions for Reflection and Discussion

1. Think of someone you know who is doubting because she or he has been influenced by false teaching. How could you gently invite this person to study the Bible with you?

2. What dangers do we face today from the influence of church leaders whose preaching has departed from the gospel?

3. How can you pray for revival in the church in Africa and prepare expectantly for God to move?

God is King

CONCLUSION
GLORY TO GOD FOR OUR ETERNAL SAFETY

To him who is able to keep you from stumbling and to present you before his glorious presence without fault and with great joy – to the only God our Saviour be glory, majesty, power and authority, through Jesus Christ our Lord, before all ages, now and for evermore! Amen (Jude 24-25).

Jude knew that his readers were in crisis. This is why, in the first part of his epistle, Jude changed his mind about writing a letter about salvation in general to instead strongly urge his readers to reject all attempts to turn them away from the gospel of Jesus Christ. Drawing on Old Testament comparisons and analogies from daily life, he vividly painted the ungodliness and immorality of the false teachers. They were condemned to judgement. I imagine that, after reading Jude's letter, his readers must have been shaken by the severity of the situation when it hit them that there were eternal consequences for departing from the gospel.

In the second part of his epistle, Jude laid out the battle plan for fighting false teaching. They needed a strong defence: protecting themselves from falling prey to falsehood. They needed a powerful offence: rescuing others from the false teachers' clutches and their doomed destiny.

I imagine Jude's readers were very alarmed. Jude had confronted them with the situation of false teaching. The false teachers seemed powerful and threatening. Jude's warnings were also firm and uncompromising. The fate of the church was at stake. What if they were not able to carry out this battle plan? What if they failed? What if they fell and couldn't make it to the finish line? They shuddered to think of the judgement they too would receive.

As you finish this book, you may have some similar concerns. We have described the urgent problem of the distortions and departures from the gospel that we face in the African church today. Perhaps you had not realized how serious the situation was. Perhaps you are worried about how you have already been influenced. Perhaps the state of the church seems so overwhelming that the situation looks hopeless to you.

This is why Jude ends his epistle with a reminder to look up. In the last two verses of his epistle, Jude assures his readers that God will preserve those who faithfully contend for the gospel and present them holy and blameless to himself at the Second Coming of Christ. His doxology sings the praises of the great Sovereign Lord who accomplishes this through Jesus Christ.

It is God who is able to keep us from stumbling. Among my Akan people of Ghana, a commonly used name for God is *Twereduampɔn*. This name literally translates as, "If you lean, or depend, on him, you will never fall." The Bible's names for God remind us of why we will never fall if we depend on him. We are depending not on our own strength to stand but on the God who appeared to Abraham as *El-Shaddai*, God Almighty (Exodus 6:3). If we are afraid that we will fall prey to false promises of wealth and health, we can remember that our needs will be met by *Jehovah-Jireh*, the Lord our provider (Genesis 22:13-14) and *Jehovah-Rapha*, the Lord who heals (Exodus 15:26).

When selfish shepherds prevail, we have *Jehovah-Ra-ah*, the Lord our shepherd (Psalm 23:1), who cares for us and models Christian leadership for those of us in ministry. When we are anxious about the state of the church, we can come to *Jehovah-Shalom*, the Lord our peace (Judges 6:24). We know he will sustain us until the victorious end of the fight because he is *Jehovah-Nissi*, the Lord our banner (Exodus 17:8-15).

Knowing God assures us deep in our beings that this is a world that our Father has made. Our dark and fallen world is beset by wars, pandemics, poverty, catastrophic climate changes, terrorist attacks, racism, dictatorships, and so much more that can keep us awake and worrying at night. Our futile and frantic efforts to control tomorrow fail. We seek meaning and hope, wrestle with guilt and shame, and feel helpless amid addictions and abuse. But the sovereign God rules over the universe in his perfect love and wisdom.

As God's children, we can therefore live with confident faith in his presence, his sufficient provision, and his adequate protection that our Father has promised to provide to us in this world (Matthew 6:33). God's love for us shines brightly through the gospel of Jesus Christ. God has gone to great lengths to make himself known to us in tangible and practical ways we can experience in our ordinary everyday lives. When we put everything in our lives in God's hand, sooner or later,

The sovereign God rules over the universe in his perfect love and wisdom.

we will begin to see God's gracious hand directing everything in our lives.

God is sovereign, the ultimate reality behind all realities.

> When we put everything in our lives in God's hand, sooner or later, we will begin to see God's gracious hand directing everything in our lives.

What's more, our eternal destiny is secure in hands much bigger than our own. Jude reminds us that we can trust "the only God our Saviour" who executed our salvation in history "through Jesus Christ our Lord" – his incarnation, death, and resurrection. We no longer need to fear facing the judgement due to sinners – being blown away or uprooted or the punishment of eternal fire. Christ has taken our eternal condemnation away. The gospel moves us from placing our trust in what we have and what we do to trusting in what God has done for us in Christ and who he says we are.

We do not need to be strong enough in our own strength to resist the battle against sin. No matter what threats we endure from suffering or the forces of evil, God is committed to our sanctification and our spiritual safety. God delights to ensure that we arrive in heaven, blameless and covered in the righteousness of Christ.

Even as we contend for the gospel, we must remember that we are not saving the gospel. The gospel is saving us. We should fight for truth, but ultimately, God has won the victory. Only God is our Saviour. God declares:

> I am God, and there is no other;
> I am God, and there is none like me.
> I make known the end from the beginning,
>   from ancient times, what is still to come.
> I say, "My purpose will stand,
>   and I will do all that I please" (Isaiah 46:9-10).

This is why Jude can't help but end on a high note. All praise and honour to Jesus Christ! He deserves glory, majesty, power, and authority. It makes me want to praise him with another name my people have for God: *Onyankopɔn*, or *Onyame*, for short, which loosely translates into English as *the high-dwelling God of ultimate satisfaction who shines brightly with glory*. That is who you are, God! Your divine radiance is glorious and majestic. You have all the power and authority to control your world and the ability to do whatever you desire!

What an exciting hope we have in the gospel! Today, let's heed Jude's inspired message. Let's turn away from false teaching and return to the gospel. As we step out boldly in faith to preach and teach the gospel, I believe our people will be redeemed and our continent transformed. Christ has secured the victory already.

May it be so, Lord Jesus!

Questions for Reflection and Discussion

1. What are some of your favourite names for God either from your own culture or from the Bible?

2. How would you encourage a fearful fellow Christian to trust God's sovereignty in ensuring the spiritual safety of his people?

3. Imagine entering God's presence physically one day, faultless and joyful. Spend some time thanking God for his power that saves us and keeps us spiritually safe. Praise God for his glory, majesty, power, and authority.

ABOUT THE AUTHOR

Reverend Canon Dr Emmanuel Kwasi Amoafo is originally from Ghana, but he lives in Kenya. He is with the Theology Departments of Global University and St. Paul's University. He has been a full-time Lecturer in Missiology and Theology at Carlile College School of Theology, Nairobi, Kenya, where he also served as the College's Director of Student Affairs.

An ordained minister, he serves in the Anglican Church of Kenya Parish of Christ Church in Westlands, Nairobi. He is also a clerical Canon at the Anglican Church of Kenya St. Luke's Cathedral, Butere Diocese, involved in the Missions, Evangelism, and Discipleship programme of the Diocese.

Passionate about the gospel, he regularly preaches in various churches throughout Kenya and abroad. He is married to Dr Esther Nkrumah and they have five young adult children.

DISSERTATION ABSTRACT

The title of my dissertation was *Contending for the Faith in the African Context: An Exegesis of Jude in Relation to Theology and Praxis in Ghana.** The purpose of this dissertation was to identify principles of biblical Christianity from an exegetical study of Jude's epistle that would be used as guidelines to advocate for contextualized biblical Christianity in five leading autonomous Pentecostal-Charismatic churches in Ghana.

In the introductory first chapter, a submission was made of the background and purpose of the study, the statement of the problem, the study's research questions, and the significance of the study. In the second chapter, the dissertation's exegetical study of Jude's message concluded that Jude's call to his readers "to contend for the faith once for all delivered to the saints" meant upholding, preserving, and persevering in seven principles of biblical Christianity, identified by the study's analysis of the text.

The third chapter examined what the social science literature reveals about the religious, socio-economic, and political factors that led to the establishment and growth of the five Ghanaian churches. It also examined the current theology and practices of these five churches. The fourth chapter submitted the study's methodological framework. That framework involved the use of

---

* This dissertation was submitted to the Doctor of Philosophy Dissertation Committee in candidacy for the degree of Doctor of Philosophy in Theological Studies at the Pan Africa Theological Seminary (PAThS: pathseminary.org). The dissertation was successfully defended on 7th June 2018.

Q-Methodology. Q-Methodology is a statistical research tool that makes the shared perceptions of a group of people observable, measurable, understandable, and communicable in research terms. In this dissertation, Q-Methodology was particularly appropriate because it enabled my research to identify, understand, review and explain the shared theological perceptions of the leaders of the churches that were the object of my research. The fifth chapter presented and analyzed the results obtained from the research data, and the sixth chapter submitted the study's conclusions and recommendations for praxis change and additional research.

By relating the essence of Jude's message to the theology and praxis of these five Ghanaian churches, the overriding aim of this dissertation was to see the churches spiritually strengthened as they apply in their various contexts the principles of biblical Christianity the study identified from Jude's epistle.

ENDNOTES

1   In the first century, the church met in the homes of its wealthier members. Philemon, a wealthy slave-owning man, hosted the church in his home in Colossae (Philemon 2b). Lydia, a businesswoman who traded in expensive purple fabric, hosted the church in Philippi in her home (Acts 16:14). Aquila and Priscilla, who ran an evidently large and profitable business that manufactured tents, hosted a church in their home (Acts 18:1-3). Gaius had a home spacious enough to host the church in his city and the means to generously host and support itinerant teachers (Romans 16:23; 3 John 1-5).

2   Itinerant Christian teachers travelled widely and freely across the far-flung Roman Empire visiting the various congregations of the New Testament church (2 Corinthians 10-11; 1 John 4:1; 2 John 10). Many of these congregations were made up of both Jewish and Gentile Christians. They generally met for three to four hours in the evenings of the first day of the week to sing, pray, share a meal together, preach, teach, and encourage one another. They had a communal Lord's Supper or "Love Feast" that affirmed the church was the family of God. These meetings bonded the early NT Christians together into a like-minded community at odds with the pagan cultures from which many of them had come. The congregations varied in size from 50-70 people. The homes of the patron hosts had dining halls with attached gardens, courtyards, or atriums that could serve large groups. See Gordon D. Fee, *The First Epistle to the Corinthians: The New International Commentary on the New Testament* (Grand Rapids, MI: Eerdmans, 1989), 531-558.

3   Charles E. Hummel, *The Prosperity Gospel: Health and Wealth and the Faith Movement* (Downers Grove, IL: InterVarsity Press, 1991), 4.

4   Hummel, *The Prosperity Gospel*, 5.

5   Gordon D. Fee and Douglas Stuart, *How to Read the Bible Book by Book: A Guided Tour* (Grand Rapids, MI: Zondervan, 2002), 425.

6   Paul Gifford, *Ghana's New Christianity: Pentecostalism in a Globalizing African Economy* (Bloomington, IN: Indiana University Press, 2004), 188.

7   Norman Anderson Sir, *Christianity and World Religions* (Leicester, UK: Inter-Varsity Press, 1984), 139-40.

8   Hans Debrunner, *A History of Christianity in Ghana* (Accra: Waterville Publishing House, 1967), 13-102.

9   Adrian Hastings, *The Church in Africa: 1450-1950* (Oxford, UK: Oxford University Press, 1996), 525-31.

10 Richard Foli, *Christianity in Ghana: A Comparative Church Growth Study* (Accra, Ghana: Trust Publications, 2006), 50-55.

11 Gifford, *Ghana's New Christianity*, 188.

12 John R. W. Stott, *The Message of Galatians* (Downers Grove, IL: Inter-Varsity Press, 1968), 126-27.

13 Unless otherwise noted, content in this paragraph and the two that follow is summarized from Robert C. Blaschke, *Quest for Power: Guidelines for Communicating the Gospel to Animists* (Katunayake, Sri Lanka: New Life Literature, 2004), 13-15, 27.

14 Philip M. Steyne, *Gods of Power: A Study of the Beliefs and Practices of Animists* (Columbia, SC: Impact International Foundation, 1999), 182-83.

15 Romans 8:29; Hebrews 2:14-18; 4:14-16.

16 Keith Ferdinando, *The Battle Is God's: Reflecting on Spiritual Warfare for African Believers* (Nairobi, Kenya: African Christian Textbooks, 2012), 13.

17 Jayson Georges, *The 3D Gospel: Ministry in Guilt, Shame, and Fear Cultures* (Timē Press, 2017), https://honorshame.com/3DGOSPEL/.

18 Timothy Keller, *Rediscovering Jonah: The Secret of God's Mercy* (New York, NY: Penguin Books, 2018), 156.

19 Warren W. Wiersbe, *The Wiersbe Bible Commentary: New Testament* (Colorado Springs, CO: David C Cook, 2007), 1024.

20 Mark R. Shaw, *The Kingdom of God in Africa: A Short History of African Christianity* (Grand Rapids, MI: Baker Books, 1998), 330.

21 Sophie de la Haye, *Byang Kato: Ambassador for Christ* (Harpenden, UK: African Christian Press, 1986), 17-22.

22 Carolyn Nystrom, "Let African Christians Be Christian Africans", *Christianity Today*, June 2009, 2. https://www.christianitytoday.com /history/2009/june/let-african-christians-be-christian-africans.html.

23 Byang H. Kato, *Biblical Christianity in Africa: A Collection of Papers and Addresses*, 1st ed, Theological Perspectives in Africa, no. 2 (Achimota, Ghana, West Africa: Africa Christian Press, 1985), 24, 31, 38.

24 Aiah Dorkuh Foday-Khabenje, "Byang Kato: Africa's Foremost Twentieth-Century Evangelical Theological Leader", *Evangelical Review of Theology* 45, no. 3 (August 2021): 204-5. Nystrom, "Let African Christians Be Christian Africans", 3.

25 Byang Kato, *Theological Pitfalls in Africa* (Nairobi, Kenya: Evangel Publishing House, 1987), 184.

26 J. Kwabena Asamoah-Gyadu, *African Charismatics: Current Developments within Indigenous Pentecostalism in Ghana* (Achimota, Ghana: Africa Christian Press, 2005), 115-120.

27 Emmanuel Kingsley Larbi, *Pentecostalism: The Eddies of Ghanaian Christianity*, Studies in African Pentecostal Christianity (Dansoman, Accra, Ghana: CPCS, 2001), 340-41.

28 Allan Heaton Anderson, *To the Ends of the Earth: Pentecostalism and the Transformation of World Christianity* (Oxford, UK: Oxford University Press, 2013), 230-34.

29 Stanley M. Burgess and Eduard M.Van Der Maas, eds., *The New International Dictionary of Pentecostal and Charismatic Movements* (Grand Rapids, MI: Zondervan, 2003), 992.

30 Hummel, *The Prosperity Gospel*, 4.

31 Paul Gifford, *African Christianity: Its Public Role* (Bloomington, IN: Indiana University Press, 1998), 91.

32 Timothy Keller, *Preaching: Communicating Faith in an Age of Skepticism* (New York, NY: Viking, 2015), 236-37.

33 Andrew Walls, "The Expansion of Christianity: An Interview with Andrew Walls," *The Christian Century* (August 2-9, 2000): 792-99, accessed March 8, 2022, https://www.religion-online.org/article/the-expansion-of-christianity-an-interview-with-andrew-walls/.

34 Albert A. Bell, Jr., *Exploring the New Testament World: An Illustrated Guide to the World of Jesus and the First Christians* (Nashville, TN: Thomas Nelson Publishers, 1998), 146.

35 Content in this paragraph comes from Ibid., 145-149.

36 Content in this paragraph comes from Ibid., 145-149.

37 Sinclair B. Ferguson, *Some Pastors and Some Teachers: Reflecting a Biblical Vision of What Every Minister Is Called to Be* (Edinburgh, UK: The Banner of Truth Trust, 2017), 363.

38 Randy J. Hedlun, "The Social Sciences and NT Interpretation", in *Backgrounds to the NT: Cultural and Historical Contexts by Carl Gibbs and Marcia Munger* (Springfield, MO: Global University, 2011), 66.

39 Ibid., 62-83.

40 Femi Adeleye, *Preachers of a Different Gospel: A Pilgrim's Reflections on Contemporary Trends in Christianity* (Grand Rapids, MI: HippoBooks, 2011), 91.

41 John Piper, "Twelve Appeals to Prosperity Preachers", in *Prosperity? Seeking the True Gospel* (Nairobi, Kenya.: African Christian Textbooks, 2015), 116-18.

42 Watchman Nee, *The Normal Christian Life* (Eastbourne, UK: Kingsway Publications, 1969), 134-35.

43 Charles W. Price, *Christ for Real: How to Grow into God's Likeness* (England, UK: Kregel Publications, 2011), 76.

44 Sinclair B. Ferguson, *Discovering God's Will* (Edinburgh, UK: The Banner of Truth Trust, 1982), 30.

45 Price, *Christ for Real*, 78-79.

46 Kenneth Hagin, *How to Write Your Own Ticket with God* (Tulsa, OK: Faith Library, 1980), 11-32.

47 Blaschke, *Quest for Power*, 77-85.

48 Price, *Christ for Real*, 225-26.

49 Jerome H. Neyrey, ed., *2 Peter, Jude: A New Translation with Introduction and Commentary*, 1st ed, The Anchor Bible, v. 37C (New York, NY: Doubleday, 1993), 75.

50 Kenneth L. Barker and John R. Kohlenberger, *Expositor's Bible Commentary: New Testament* (Grand Rapids, MI: Zondervan, 1994), 1122.

51 Dieudonné Tamfu, *The Gods of the Prosperity Gospel: Unmasking American Idols in Africa*, 2020, 1, https://www.desiringgod.org /articles/the-gods-of-the-prosperity-gospel.

52 "Police arrest man who burnt church property after failing to get out of poverty", *The Daily Monitor*, 16 March 2020, 1-2, https://www.monitor.co.ug/News/National/church-property-man -Police-arrested-burnt-poverty/688334-5493272-y0wkfuz/index.html.

53 Gifford, *Ghana's New Christianity*, 40-41.

54 Wanjohi Githae, "Tough Laws to Now Tame Rogue Clergy", *Sunday Nation*, 3 January 2016, 1.

55 Ibid., 4.

56 Blaschke, *Quest for Power*, 71-72.

57 Luke 10:17-19; Ephesians 1:20-22; 1 John 4:4; 5:18.

58 Ferdinando, *The Battle Is God's*, 13.

59 Ibid., 83.

60 Timothy Keller, *The Prodigal God* (New York, NY: Penguin Books, 2008), 130-131. Keller, *Preaching*, 239.

61 Gifford, *Ghana's New Christianity*, 63.

62 Paul Gifford, "Ghana's Charismatic Churches," *Journal of Religion in Africa* 24, no. 3 (1994): 241-65 https://doi.org/10.2307/1581301.

63 Timothy Keller, *Counterfeit Gods: The Empty Promises of Money, Sex, and Power, and the Only Hope That Matters* (New York, NY: Penguin Books, 2009), xix-xx.

64 Joseph Quayesi-Amakye, "A Yeast in the Flour: Pentecostalism as the African Realisation of the Gospel", *UNISA Studia Historiae Ecclesiasticae* 42, no. 3 (2016): 71-84.

65 Timothy Keller and Katherine Leary Alsdorf, *Every Good Endeavour: Connecting Your Work to God's Work*, (New York, NY: Penguin Books, 2012), 37.

66 Ibid., 55.

67 J. I. Packer, *Keep in Step with the Spirit: Finding Fullness in Our Walk with God* (Grand Rapids, MI: Baker Books, 2005), 186.

68 Gifford, *Ghana's New Christianity*, 70.

69 J. Kwabena Asamoah-Gyadu, *Sighs and Signs of the Spirit: Ghanaian Perspectives on Pentecostalism and Renewal in Africa* (Oxford, UK: Regnum Africa, 2015), 167.

70 John R. W. Stott, *Christian Mission in the Modern World* (London, UK: Falcon Books, 1975), 27.

71 Murray W. Dempster, "Evangelism, Social Concern and the Kingdom of God", in *Called and Empowered: Global Mission in Pentecostal Perspective* (Peabody, MA: Hendrickson Publishers, 2008), 38.

72 The exegesis of this Mark 11 passage is drawn from Tim Keller, *Jesus the King: Understanding the Life and Death of the Son of God*, (New York, NY: Penguin Books, 2016), 174-76.

73 Walter C. Wright Jr., *Relational Leadership: A Biblical Model for Influence and Service* (Bucks, UK: Paternoster Press, 2000), 183.

74 Norman Hillyer, *1 & 2 Peter, Jude* (Grand Rapids, MI: Baker Books, 1992), 255.

75 N. T. Wright, *Colossians and Philemon: An Introduction and Commentary*, Tyndale New Testament Commentaries, v. 12 (Nottingham, England; Downers Grove, IL: Inter-Varsity Press; IVP Academic, 2008), 94.

76 For a fuller discussion see J. I. Packer, *A Passion for Holiness* (Nottingham, UK: Crossway Books, 1992), 215.

77 This illustration comes from Sinclair B. Ferguson, *Children of the Living God* (Edinburgh, UK: Banner of Truth Trust, 1989), 118.

78 Keller, *Preaching*, 119.

79 Ibid., 239-40.

80 Keller, *Jesus the King*, 229.

81 Keller, *Preaching*, 51.

82 Ibid.

83 Timothy Keller, *Hope in Times of Fear: The Resurrection and the Meaning of Easter* (New York, NY: Viking, 2021), 110-11.

84 Keller, *Preaching*, 9-23.

85 Sinclair Ferguson, *Preaching Christ from the OT: Developing a Christ-Centred Instinct* (London, UK: Proclamation Trust Media, 2000), 1-17.

86 Haddon W. Robinson, *Biblical Preaching: The Development and Delivery of Expository Messages*, Third Edition (Grand Rapids, MI: Baker Academic, A Division of Baker Publishing Group, 2014), 17-32.

87 Ibid.

88 Keller, *Preaching*, 237-38.

89 Donald C. Stamps, *The NIV Full Study Bible* (Grand Rapids, MI: Zondervan Publishing House, 1992), 1506.

90 Ibid.

91 Joseph Quayesi-Amakye, "Prophetic Practices in Contemporary Pentecostalism in Ghana", *Canadian Journal of Pentecostal-Charismatic Christianity* 6 (2015): 57.

92 See also John Musyimi, *A Counterfeit Gospel* (Nairobi, Kenya: Publish4All, 2016), 143.

93 Unless otherwise noted, the content in the next five paragraphs comes from Quayesi-Amakye, "Prophetic Practices in Contemporary Pentecostalism in Ghana": 43-69.

94 Miriam Adeney, *Kingdom Without Borders: The Untold Story of Global Christianity* (Downers Grove, IL: IVP Books, 2009), 101-2.

95 Ferdinando, *The Battle Is God's*, 22.

96 Ibid., 102.

97 Quayesi-Amakye, "Prophetic Practices in Contemporary Pentecostalism in Ghana", 43-69.

98 Price, *Christ for Real*, 176.

99 This and the following two paragraphs that explain the fruit of the Spirit and its effects in our Christian lives summarize what is said by Charles Price, *Christ for Real*, 110-114.

100 James D. G. Dunn, *Jesus and the Spirit: A Study of the Religious and Charismatic Experiences of Jesus and the First Christians as Reflected in the New Testament* (London, UK: SCM Press, 1975), 245-46.

101 Packer, *Keep in Step with the Spirit*, 144.

102 This description of the sounds of Accra is inspired by Marleen de Witte, "Accra's Sounds and Sacred Spaces", *International Journal of Urban and Regional Research* 32, No. 3 (September 2008): 700.

103 Paul G. Hiebert, R. Daniel Shaw, and Tite Tienou, "Responding to Split-Level Christianity and Folk Religion," *International Journal of Frontier Missions* 16, no. 4 (October 1999): 7.

104 J. I. Packer, *Weakness Is the Way* (Wheaton, IL: Crossway, 2013), 89.

105 Ibid., J. D. Douglas and Merrill C. Tenney, *New International Bible Dictionary* (Grand Rapids, MI: Zondervan, 1987), 448.

106 Emmanuel Kingsley Larbi, *Pentecostalism*, 424-25.

107 Erik Raymond, *The Soft Prosperity Gospel*, 2014, 1, https://www.ligonier.org/learn/articles/soft-prosperity-gospel/.

108 Packer, *Weakness Is the Way*, 102.

109 Kenneth L. Barker and Larry L. Walker, "Zechariah" in *The NIV Study Bible* ed., Kenneth Barker (Grand Rapids, MI: Zondervan, 2011), 1548.

110 Jones Darkwa Amanor, "Pentecostalism in Ghana: An African Reformation," *Cyberjournal for Pentecostal-Charismatic Research* 13, No. 1 (2008): 2-5, www.pctii.org/cyberj/cyberj13/amanor.html.

111 Christopher J. H. Wright, *The Mission of God: Unlocking the Bible's Grand Narrative* (Downers Grove, IL: IVP Academic, 2006), 62.

112 J. E. Church, *Quest for the Highest: A Diary of the East African Revival* (Exeter, UK: Paternoster Press, 1981), 130-137.

113 Colin C. Whittaker, *Great Revivals: When God Moves in Power* (Springfield, MO: Gospel Publishing House, 1984), 21-22.

114 Colin Reed, *Walking in the Light: Reflections on the East African Revival and Its Link to Australia* (Victoria, Australia: Acorn Press, 2007), 10.

115 Ibid., 12.

116 Kevin Ward and Emma Wild-Wood, *The East African Revival: History and Legacies* (Surrey, UK: Ashgate Publishing Ltd, 2012), 3-7.

117 Mark R. Shaw, *Global Awakening: How 20th-Century Revivals Triggered a Christian Revolution* (Downers Grove, IL: IVP Academic, 2010), 93-111.

118 Reed, *Walking in the Light*, 10.

119 Ibid., 12.

120 Ibid., iii.

121 Whittaker, *Great Revivals*, 25-125.

122 Selwyn Hughes, *Revival: Times of Refreshing* (Surrey, UK: CWR, 2004), 14.

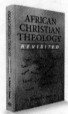

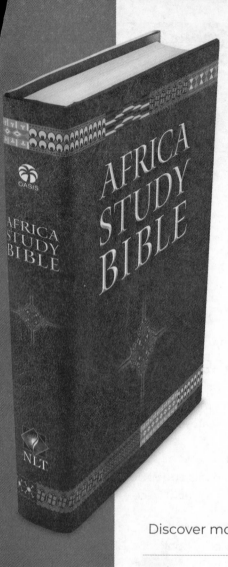